Dear Becky,

I hope you enjoy this book about "True and Constant Friends".

Thank you for your friendship my true and constant friend.

Merry Christmas,

Belinda
2018

# TRUE *and* CONSTANT FRIENDS

# TRUE *and* CONSTANT FRIENDS

Love *and* Inspiration
*from* Our Grandmothers,
Mothers, *and* Friends

## Kelley Paul

CENTER
STREET

New York  Nashville  Boston

Center Street
Hachette Book Group
1290 Avenue of the Americas
New York, NY 10104

www.CenterStreet.com

Book design by Michael Hentges

Printed in the United States of America
WOR
First edition: April 2015   10 9 8 7 6 5 4 3 2 1

Center Street is a division of Hachette Book Group, Inc.
The Center Street name and logo are trademarks of Hachette Book Group, Inc.

The Hachette Speakers Bureau provides a wide range of authors for speaking events.
To find out more, go to www.HachetteSpeakersBureau.com or call 866-376-6591.

Library of Congress Cataloging-in-Publication data has been applied for.

ISBN: 978-1-4555-6075-2 (hardcover ed.); ISBN: 978-1-4789-8786-4 (Audiobook down-loadable ed.); ISBN: 978-1-4555-6074-5 (Ebook ed.)

# CONTENTS

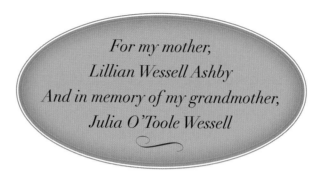

*For my mother,*
*Lillian Wessell Ashby*
*And in memory of my grandmother,*
*Julia O'Toole Wessell*

## Acknowledgments

To Brigid Elsken Galloway, Meg Waters Lambert, Blair Gatewood Norman, Kathleen Albritton Fittro, Margaret Bryan French, and Sevgi, thank you for sharing your memories and lives with me. I am honored by the generous, enthusiastic way you each responded to this project, and the eighteen months we have spent laughing and crying over your stories has deepened our friendship as well as the love and respect I have for you all.

I owe special gratitude to you, Brigid, for not only reading and commenting on many of my first drafts, but also for discovering HomeFront and its wonderful ArtSpace gallery online, the source of the paintings in this book. As you wrote to me so many years ago: thank you, my true and constant friend.

Thank you, Loretta, for sharing your story with me. You are a woman of extraordinary strength and faith, as was your beautiful daughter Kela.

To my dear friend Alicia, thanks for your patient computer and technical help, and for being the keeper of my passwords, in so many ways.

To my dad, Hilton, thank you for running behind me until I pedaled fast enough, and then letting me fly. You are the best father in the world. And to my sons William, Duncan and Robert, and my brothers Jeff and David, I am grateful for your inspiration, support and love.

To my husband Rand, thank you for your steadfast belief in me, and for more than two and half decades of love, laughter, and surprises. You are brave, and you make me more so. I love you.

Finally, to Kate Hartson, my brilliant, insightful, and energetic editor at Hachette, I cannot begin to express the depth of my gratitude for your boundless encouragement and faith in this book. Working with you has truly been an experience I will remember forever, and I treasure your friendship.

# Foreword
By Senator Rand Paul

Vincent Remini

Kelley has always been a writer. Whether writing marketing literature for the telecommunications industry or for her own creative expression, it has been a constant in her life. During my medical training at Duke, she was our main breadwinner, writing for companies in Research Triangle Park. Even when the subject matter was less than scintillating, she had a gift for making it so.

Since I entered politics, Kelley is always the first reviewer I seek for my speeches and articles, and she always makes them better. As our sons and friends will attest, she is also a good storyteller, so when she told me that she wanted to write about her relationships with her grandmother, mother and close-knit group of college friends, I knew it would be great.

As you know real men don't cry, or at least they don't usually admit to it but, as I read Kelley's essays, I laughed, I cried, and I was moved. The running joke in our family is that she is such a great storyteller that we weren't sure if she was writing fiction or non-fiction, but the truth is that she always makes real life much more interesting – sometimes more interesting in the telling than perhaps it was in the living!

Kelley is convinced that her storytelling gene comes from the Irish grandmother she writes about in this book, but I think she got a healthy dose from her father Hilton too—he can tell a story you've heard a hundred times and still reel you in for the climax.

My family may count fewer dramatic storytellers in our ranks, but it's not that we don't have a story to tell. In this book, Kelley writes of the powerful sources of inspiration our mothers and grandmothers are, and in the Paul family that is certainly true.

The women in my family have been long-lived, strong-willed and opinionated. From my grandmothers to my mother runs a strength and direction that has guided our family for generations. Even during times in history when women didn't often take leadership roles in society, the women in my family were the quiet, yet powerful directors of our destiny. In the winter of 1903, my maternal great-grandmother Millicent Duncan Creed wrote over one hundred letters to her fiancé Herman. She described great snowfalls and twenty-two degrees below zero weather. She described exhilarating sleigh rides and buggy rides and how much more delightful they would have been with him by her side.

Herman worked in a sawmill about sixty miles away. In those days, before automobiles, it was a major undertaking to travel that far and so he returned only on holidays. The train took her letters to him. Her letters warned him not to have too much fun or pay too much attention to the German girls there. She wrote of Sabbath Day School, sermons, and lectures. Often, she wrote of missing church because of quarantine for smallpox or measles or muddy, impassable roads.

I was surprised that Millicent wrote about a new card game that was "all the rage" and helped alleviate their cabin fever during the harsh winter. When she had visited us down in Texas in her late eighties, we were told that she strongly disapproved of cards and had never played. We took particular delight in corrupting her with a game of Old Maid. Little did we know then that she had once upon a time, in her rebellious youth, enjoyed a good game of cards. But we didn't stop there. We also took my great-grandmother to her first movie, *Chitty Chitty Bang Bang*, which she loved. Oh, the rebellious influence of children in the seventies!

In addition to Millicent's letters in 1903–1904, Herman's mother wrote occasionally. She was ill with chronic symptoms of age, but her strong faith gave her comfort. She wrote this to Herman in March of 1904:

> "Our Sabbath was lovely which I spent at home as usual. But the dear Lord willing I hope I can soon go to His house again. Anyway His grace is sufficient for me. There is a song in my soul today, a blessed sunshine that no outward circumstances can take away. The Lord is a sun and a shield to all that trust in him. May he always be your guide."

Their families were not rich but they were literate and spiritual. My great-grandmother Millicent did not attend college but her sister graduated from North Eastern Ohio Normal School in 1908. Millicent, like her mother before her, was active in the Women's Christian Temperance Union of Mahoning County, Ohio. In 1874, the temperance crusade began in Ohio and the first national convention of the Woman's Christian Temperance Union was held in Cleveland.

According to family lore, they sang in the prisons against the devil's liquor rum. We have no record of their involvement in women's suffrage but the Temperance Union officially endorsed women's suffrage as a way of gaining more participation and influence for women. I don't think Millicent and her mother were of the Carry Nation variety of temperance activists—to my knowledge they confined their protest tactics to singing, not hatchets.

Millicent was an activist to the end. I remember listening to her interrogate my father at her one-hundredth birthday party back in 1984 about sending AWACS (advanced surveillance planes) to Egypt. My father had been a "no" vote in congress and, fortunately for him, my great-grandmother approved.

She was tireless in her efforts to register people to vote—even working to register more than one hundred fellow residents at her assisted living facility. As the descendant of abolitionists and temperance workers, I think she tried to register only Republicans.

The women in my family were a force to be reckoned with because of their faith, energy, and intelligence, but also sheer longevity. Millicent's grandmother, Sarah Millicent Rose Howard, was born in 1836 and was still going strong at age eighty-seven, until she stepped out of a jitney and was struck by a car in 1923. My mother treasures a quilt knitted by Sarah, whom they called Ma Howard.

My mother's mother, Carol Creed Wells, graduated from Ohio University in the early 1930s at a time when few women went to college, much less graduated. Kelley and I have a framed picture of her in the foyer of our home that never fails to draw the notice of guests. In the photo she is sitting, knees bent, aiming a rifle at a distant target, a row of carbines in the background.

Carol, or Gram as we knew her, was not quite the teetotaler her mother was. She loved parties, joined a sorority, and was a bit of a rule breaker. As kids we loved the stories she told us of my grandfather climbing in the second story window of her dormitory, long after visiting hours for boys had ended.

Gram was an avid coin collector and spent hours with me as a child, sorting coins and peering at mint marks. As time went on, her vision began to fail and I became her eyes, spying the faintness of marks on weather worn coins. I went with her to the eye surgeon as her cataracts were removed, then her corneas replaced, and, finally, when we received the sad news that macular degeneration had irreparably damaged her retinas. Those trips to the ophthalmologist with her were among the reasons I ultimately decided to become an eye surgeon.

My father's mother, Margaret Dumont Paul, finished high school while her husband finished only eight grades. My dad says that without her management and accounting skills, the family dairy business would never have thrived to become the main milk delivery enterprise in Carnegie and Greentree, Pennsylvania.

Even after long days working at the dairy and caring for five sons, Margaret found time to help those less fortunate than she. She delivered Meals on Wheels to invalids and shut-ins well into her eighties. Even after she was crippled with her own arthritis and maladies, she would carry meals up long winding stairs to houses perched in the hilly sections of south Pittsburgh.

My grandmother lived in an era when every penny was counted and cataloged, lights were never burned without a purpose, the tap water was not allowed to run continuously when washing dishes, and buying new clothes only occurred when the old ones were worn out.

I interviewed my grandmother when she was ninety about her work in the family dairy business and as a volunteer for the American Bible Society. She spoke of taking the trolley to downtown Pittsburgh to deliver Bibles to an African American church. Although we sometimes assume race relations were far superior in the northern cities before the Civil Rights Movement, the truth is that separation de facto existed in the north as well. Her trip to downtown Pittsburgh, especially alone, was considered daring at the time. She never told her husband of seventy years about delivering those Bibles.

Grandmother Margaret lived in a time when, by all appearances, the men in the family made the decisions, but there was always a hint that the men could never have made the right decisions without her help. She was not boastful but it was always clear that she was confident of her abilities.

My mother, Carol Wells Paul, followed in her mother's footsteps to Ohio University. My father went to Gettysburg College and my mother, just like her grandmother Millicent, wrote hundreds of letters to her beau during those years apart (those letters were pointedly not made available to the author).

My mother would have succeeded at any career she chose. She would be the first to say that her decision to devote her life to raising, organizing, feeding, and clothing her five children was the career she chose enthusiastically and should not be viewed as somehow a deprivation of another path.

But, as times changed, so did our family. Today, my sisters work both outside the home and inside the home. My older sister Lori is a bookkeeper and mother of five, and my younger sister Joy is an OB-GYN and mother of six. Two of my nieces are physicians and one is in veterinary school.

Barbara Tuchman writes of how the American Revolution opened up progress to people from all walks of life, not just the nobility. Think of what has been lost over the centuries by restricting leadership in government and society to only men of nobility. And take that one step further: Imagine what progress has been lost by excluding women and minorities from positions of leadership.

I believe we all have reason to be hopeful about the future as both men and women, of all backgrounds, races, and creeds are encouraged to excel to their maximum potential. Nothing illustrates that viewpoint better than the stories of inspiring women in this book, whose courage, perseverance and optimism define the American spirit.

—Rand Paul

# Brushstrokes of Hope
## The Story of the Art

The paintings in this book are original works of art created by the women of the HomeFront Family Preservation Center in Lawrence, New Jersey. Every day, HomeFront changes lives by providing refuge and hope to homeless mothers and their children.

Many of the women at HomeFront have struggled with addiction, violence, and abuse. And yet once in a supportive, healthy environment that offers them and their children a safe haven, these same women have been able to express themselves through artwork that is hopeful, thoughtful, and life affirming.

The paintings are a testament to both the transformative work of this organization and the redemptive power of art.

I was excited to be able to share their beautiful paintings in this book, as they provide a visual echo to the overriding theme of each chapter—that beneath the most ordinary or broken surface, we all have a unique and inspiring story to tell.

"*Each friend represents a world in us, a world not born until they arrive, and it is only by this meeting that a new world is born.*"

Anaïs Nin, *Diary of Anaïs Nin, Vol. 1*

*chapter one*

# By Chance We Met

Kathy Bird

"It is by chance that we met,
by choice that we became friends."

ANONYMOUS

For more than thirty years, I have been friends with six women. We met in the autumn of 1981 as freshmen at Rhodes College in Memphis, Tennessee, and despite living in different states across the country, we have faithfully reunited for a long weekend nearly every year since graduation.

This year we all reached a milestone birthday, so we expanded our reunion into a weeklong beach celebration worthy of thirty-two years of sharing stories we know by heart but still make us laugh. Perhaps it was turning fifty, perhaps it was an introspection borne of suddenly living my life in the public eye, but this year I felt a keener understanding of just how powerful and precious these enduring friendships are to me.

Even though we are geographically scattered, we have remained in touch by phone, email and our treasured annual reunion since our graduation in 1985. Like all women, we have failed and succeeded, celebrated and mourned, and kept on going. We are from varied backgrounds and faiths, and we have different points of view on many things. But to each of us, our friendship is something sparkling and fine.

We have stood up for one another at our weddings, shared countless photographs of our beautiful children and families, and cheered our successes in career and love and life. We have sustained one another through life's hard and dark times—divorce, the alcoholism of a spouse, autism, difficulties with children and loved ones, disease, and the sudden loss of parents and a precious sister. Through it all, we have been a balm for sorrow and despair, or just made one another laugh, often at the same

time. Whether it's a cup of coffee, a casserole at the door, or a calm, trusted voice on the phone, real friends have an instinct for what is necessary in the moment.

I consider it one of life's greatest blessings to have true and constant friends, the kind that you both weather and savor life's seasons with. Over the past decades, the questions and topics have certainly changed—at eighteen the conversations usually began with "What do you think he meant by that?" and "Why hasn't he called?" In other words, it was all about the boys.

This was the 1980s, long before cell phones and social media. We had to make commitments for "real dates" well in advance, and wait for (or have the courage to make) phone calls on landlines, something our own children can't even imagine. There was no expectation of an immediate text response to a chance meeting or flirtation, and there was more patience and vulnerability involved for all parties. But looking back and, at the risk of sounding like an old lady, I'll say it: I think it was better then.

Our friendships helped make the drama of the dating game less excruciating, and we soothed one another's broken hearts over pitchers of margaritas, chips and salsa, and lots of unkind laughter as we made fun of the cad's nose or how he really did look kind of funny when he ran (which was occasionally awkward when the couple got back together).

By our mid-twenties, the conversations had evolved into a heady, utterly self-centered mix of career aspirations and relationships, still heavily weighted toward romance because that's always more exciting to discuss with your girlfriends. We toasted new jobs and promotions, analyzed the smart but quirky guy we met at the airport, and the personality disorder of the terrible boss. We fixed each other up with cute coworkers and, in this category, I get to take credit for one happy marriage—okay, I was technically introducing Blair to Steve's *friend*, but they wouldn't have met without my Emma-like interventions!

> *"The older we get, the more we understand that the women who know and love us—and love us despite what they know about us—are the joists that hold up the house of our existence."*    Anna Quindlen, *Lots of Candles, Plenty of Cake*

In our thirties and forties, kids entered the fray and we rejoiced and commiserated over the often-overwhelming experience of motherhood. We one-upped each other with graphic labor and delivery dramas and embarrassing potty-training disasters, gleefully scorned the hyper-competitive sports moms, and traded notes on how to secretly lurk on our teens' Facebook and Instagram accounts. Through it all, a great sense of humor and an appreciation of the absurd have connected us through our shared experiences. That, and knowing when to keep your mouth shut!

Speaking of maintaining a sense of humor, my husband Rand's campaign for the US Senate (after nearly twenty years as a doctor in peaceful Bowling Green, Kentucky) certainly required that of me. Raising a family amid the contact sport of American politics, I have had to call on reserves of strength and calm that I didn't realize I had, and I've leaned hard on my friends.

I've also found guidance and courage in my faith, my family, and even my history. As I grow older, I can feel the experiences of my mother and grandmother resonating in me, giving me a new sense of bravery and purpose. The lifetime of anecdotes, stories, and family lore passed down from my mother, aunts, and grandmother have become more meaningful and real to me now.

Just remembering my grandmother Julia's joyful smile as she greeted me with a merry "'Tis Herself!" in her musical Irish accent never fails to fill me with a sense of optimism and assurance. She was a small woman who lived a life that might appear hard and humble from the outside, but her heart and her hopes were huge, and they inspire me still. I feel a little flame of faith and hopefulness every time I remember her, and it makes me wonder if there are more than genes woven into the strands of our DNA— aren't the stories and inspiration of our loved ones, their pain and joy and wisdom, woven into us as well?

So this year, I asked each friend for a favor before we met for our reunion. Tell me a story, I asked each of them. Tell me about a woman who has influenced you, guided you, and fostered your sense of joy, of possibility, of courage. I love these women, my friends. They are each extraordinary. And after more than three decades of friendship, I wanted to find out just what was woven into their DNA. I had an unshakeable feeling that their mothers and grandmothers would have experiences and histories that were fascinating and inspiring.

I was right, and that is the genesis of this book. It is a tender salute to Julia O'Toole Wessell, my Irish immigrant grandmother, who had only an eighth-grade education and worked as a maid for most of her life, but who lived her American dream with an unsinkable optimism and verve that I feel in my very bones. I try to live my life in a way that reflects her faith and buoyant spirit. It is a toast to my dear friends, both those who appear in this book and others, whose lives have intersected mine and made it stronger, finer, truer. And it is a tribute to my beloved mother, Lillian Ashby, who is—always—my touchstone.

The women in these stories, while from a range of backgrounds

and cultural experiences, share traits of courage, faith, optimism and an unconquerable love of family. They are the Mississippi matriarch who, at age thirty, built a school for disabled children next to her home and helped to found a new church at eighty; the Turkish coffee girl who dared to sail across the ocean to define her own future; and the quiet mother who stayed up nights sewing a prom dress just like the one in the store her daughter dreamed of, but she could not afford to buy. They are our mothers and grandmothers: our first and most powerful sources of love and inspiration, the keystones on which we, so fragile at first, are constructed.

One of the wonderful surprises of writing this book was that, once I got the conversation started, each friend had a truly extraordinary and compelling figure in her life whose story begged to be told, even if on the surface she appeared to be just an everyday woman—a mother or grandmother, but nobody special.

To accompany each story, I've also selected quotes and poetry from some of my literary heroines, the writers and characters that have fueled my imagination since early childhood. I have been in love with books

> *"Remember well, and bear in mind,*
> *a constant friend is hard to find."*
> Laura Ingalls Wilder
> *Farm Journalist: Writings from the Ozarks*

since I was a very young girl. Some of my earliest, sweetest memories are of my mother taking me to the library as a preschooler, and the way those books felt as I clutched them in my arms, their musty smell tickling my nose and hinting at all the secret worlds and beautiful pictures I would find inside.

My first literary heroine was Laura Ingalls Wilder, from whom I learned early lessons in bravery and resilience. In elementary school, I read and re-read her Little House on the Prairie books until the spines cracked. During Saturday sleepovers, my best friend Lally and I would create a cozy cabin in the basement of her house and play "Pioneer" for hours, rocking our baby Carrie by the fire in between dangerous treks into the Big Woods (a dark hall lined with old water skis) to help Pa fight off vicious panthers and bears.

I have included Laura Ingalls Wilder, along with many of my favorite writers, from Charlotte Brontë to Barbara Kingsolver, in this book. Like my friends, and like their mothers and grandmothers, they are diverse in outlook and experience but singular in that I have learned from, and been inspired by, them all.

I hope that these stories, poems and quotes will not only inspire you, but also remind you of a woman in your own life—a mother, a grandmother, an aunt, a sister or a friend. I believe that if we take the time to listen, everyone has an intriguing story to tell, a truth to unveil, or a lesson to teach. Too often we don't recognize the significance of our teacher in the moment. Sometimes, her gifts are only revealed when we remember her.

Gennie Darisme

"…My parents, and librarians along the way, taught me about the space between words; about the margins, where so many juicy moments of life and spirit and friendship could be found."

Anne Lamott

*Plan B: Further Thoughts on Faith*

Kathy Bird

*chapter two*

# Hope

Hope is the thing with feathers —
That perches in the soul —
And sings the tune without the words —
And never stops — at all —

And sweetest — in the Gale — is heard —
And sore must be the storm —
That could abash the little Bird
That kept so many warm —

I've heard it in the chillest land —
And on the strangest Sea —
Yet — never — in Extremity,
It asked a crumb — of me.

*Emily Dickinson*

# Grandma Julia, My Irish Blessing

*"Above all, be the heroine of your life, not the victim."*

*Nora Ephron*
Wellesley Class of 1996 Commencement Address

My beloved grandmother, Julia O'Toole Wessell, came to this country from Ireland in 1929 at age nineteen. She sailed alone across the Atlantic on a ship called the Adriatic, part of the famous White Star Line, which included the Titanic. As a little girl, I loved to hear Grandma tell stories of her dangerous and exciting journey. She was a natural storyteller (and honestly a bit of an exaggerator, as all good storytellers are) and she kept me spellbound with tales told in her musical Irish brogue.

Julia set off from her small village of Dun Laoghaire alone, leaving behind her parents and younger siblings, Mae and Denis. Dun Laoghaire is a beautiful little seaport town, and my grandmother loved to tell how the English troops landed there during the Easter Rebellion of 1916 and marched into Dublin. My great-grandmother, Catherine Fitzpatrick, went into labor with her youngest daughter Mae the day the troops came ashore, and Julia, just a tiny girl of six, had to run out into the streets filled with marching English soldiers to fetch the doctor.

As an adult, I understood that Grandma came to this country fleeing poverty (her father was an invalid, having been exposed to mustard gas as a soldier during World War I). But listening to her stories as a child, I would never have known that. Julia O'Toole was an incredibly proud woman—no matter her circumstances, she always viewed her experiences, past and present, in the rosiest possible light.

In her stories of her voyage on the White Star Line, she sounded more like a movie star or heiress than a poor girl traveling alone with little more than the clothes on her back and a bit of money pinned to her underwear. From her life, I have learned many things, but the one that has served me best is to put on some lipstick and laugh at circumstance whenever you can (even after a good cry).

Grandma was a bit of a snob about the fact that she had a sponsor in the United States, her Aunt Nora, who worked as a laundress in New York City and saved enough to pay her passage in third class on the *Adriatic*. This meant that she did not have to travel in steerage, nor did she have to suffer the indignities of Ellis Island.

"I had a sponsor, don't you know, Kelley," she would say to me in confiding tones, shaking a be-ringed finger so I understood the gravity and importance of such a thing. "I was not in steerage with the rest of the rabble. I was not with the likes of them. We had gay dances and parties. Oh, the dances! I was lovely, a lovely lass like you, and my feet were never at rest with all the dancing. The handsome gentlemen were lined up for me to dance with them!"

Grandma was a bit vain about her looks, and especially so in retrospect. From her descriptions, her younger self sounded a bit like a cross between Grace Kelly and Marilyn Monroe. While this is not exactly confirmed in her photos, her creative license was one of the many things I adored about her nonetheless. As I said, she put a positive spin on everything!

WHITE STAR LINE
TWIN-SCREW R.M.S. "ADRIATIC."

My favorite part of her voyage story was when she was crowned "Miss White Star Line" on the final night of her journey. My grandmother was so charming and outgoing that she had befriended all of the employees on the ship, and they wanted to make her last evening special. "At the 3rd Class Costume Ball I was dressed as Miss White Star Line," she would tell me, eyes shining with the memory. "The chambermaids all got together and pinned monogrammed napkins all over my dress and created a gorgeous, elaborate headpiece for me. I won first prize! We were all in high spirits, as we would be docking into America the next day. Everyone was talking about sailing past the Statue of Liberty, seeing it shining ahead on the water. Oh, the excitement on the ship, Kelley! My heart was pounding as I danced. It was thrilling to be nineteen, a beautiful young girl, and beginning my adventures in the greatest country on earth."

My grandparents,
Julia and Harry,
on their wedding day.

Listening to her stories as a teenager, I was in awe of her bravery: traveling alone at such a young age with no way to ever reach her family if she needed them. It was dangerous, romantic, the stuff of novels—and I ate it up. Grandma was always being pursued by handsome "rogues and devils." "Of course I had to put a stop to their fresh ways, don't you know," she'd tell me with a wink.

She had left behind a fiancé, Boxer Byrne, a soldier who was "black Irish handsome" and mad for her. I always felt a little sorry for Boxer, who was devastated by her headstrong departure for America, leaving him heartbroken and alone. The story went that after Grandma left, all the O'Tooles would take cover when they saw Boxer approaching. He'd come up to them, red-faced and bellowing, "Where's Julia?" I always hoped that he'd found a new fiancée after that.

Her first job was as a live-in maid at the mansion of the owners of the Saks Fifth Avenue store. According to my Aunt Julie, this is where she developed her love of fashion and home décor, which lasted all of her life. As she recalls, "She adapted well after she learned the ropes and, when looking for the dumbwaiter, knew to look for a contraption in the hall, not a speechless man!"

She was provided with a safe and comfortable room, good food, some time off, and was able to attend Mass. She missed her family terribly and sent money home to Ireland every month, something she did her entire life, even after she married and had children, when she could spare only a few dollars at a time.

Her work as a live-in maid provided her a ready-made social life that eased her homesickness, as there were lots of other young women working in the house that she befriended. Grandma loved to tell stories of how she and the other girls would flirt with the delivery boys in the markets and make dates to meet them on various New York street corners. They would go up to the top floor of the mansion and peek to see if the boys would show up!

A year or two after her arrival in the United States, Grandma contracted rheumatic fever and became very ill. She was terrified that her employers would find out that she was sick, and went to great lengths to conceal her illness from them. "I would have been deported if I could not work, don't you know, and sent back to Ireland, which was a mark of great shame. I would have been a burden on the state," she would tell me gravely.

For some reason her rheumatic fever stories always featured her crawling downstairs in a weakened state before the family awakened in order to secretly drink water from the flower vases because of her terrible, unquenchable thirst. I never quite understood that one but it certainly increased the drama factor in her story!

When she became very ill, her employer, a kind woman, did not fire her or have her deported but sent her to a hospital. To aid in her recovery, the woman then sent Grandma to her summer home in Deal Beach, New Jersey, to spend a month by the ocean. She rode all the way to the coast in an open roadster, driven by the son of the family. Grandma loved it, of course!

## Grandma's Visits

All during my childhood and teens, Grandma gave me wonderful, glittering things when she would visit from New York. Just the words New York

conjured images of glamour and sophistication for me. She brought me her old purses and costume jewelry she no longer wore—the bigger the better, as far as I was concerned. I can probably blame her for my purse obsession. Photographs of me riding my tricycle at age three feature a large lady's handbag circa 1945 draped over the handlebars. Even at three I could not venture down the driveway without my bag!

Grandma's precious castoffs always had a great story behind them.

"Oh, Kelley, Mrs. Werthheimer gave this one to me the summer I was twenty-one and I carried it the night I met your grandfather at Gristedes Market and we went out for a chocolate malted together. I looked quite stylish and your grandfather was so handsome with his gorgeous Swedish hair and dimpled chin." Everything Mrs. Werthheimer and Mrs. Roskin gave Grandma was "fine, fine" and "only the best." Grandma's employers were wealthy women, or as she liked to say in awed tones with a raised eyebrow, "high society."

As a little girl I loved all the heavy purses and glittering, colorful necklaces and brooches, and I would accessorize my Sears T-shirts and shorts with multiple elegant "jewels." When I was fifteen, Grandma gave me a small beaded evening purse, which I prize to this day. It is covered in intricate ivory glass beads and seed pearls, with a sparkling design fashioned of crystal buttons at the clasp. Inside is a beautiful cream lining of pure silk.

I was dazzled by it. I can still see Grandma's shining face as she pressed it into my hands, voice hushed with significance. Have I mentioned that she loved to make a production of everything? "Now this, Kelley, is very special indeed, and I have been waiting for you to be old enough to have it," she said. "It's from a very fine store in New York and Mrs. Roskin gave it to me to carry when your grandfather and I went to The Top of the World Lodge for cocktails and dinner on our wedding anniversary. I want you to have it, and promise me you'll carry it to wonderful parties and dances where I know you will be the belle of the ball!"

And she went on to describe her elegant employer carrying this "fine, fine" purse to the ballet and the opera, and to all the beautiful charity balls and sparkling parties she attended in New York. I was fifteen then, and for the first time my attention shifted from the wealthy society ladies and their fabulous castoffs to my grandmother herself.

My entire life I had listened to Grandma's tales of Mrs. Wertheimer and Mrs. Roskin, whom she "worked for," but until that moment it had never really occurred to me to ask her what she actually did. I was too dazzled by the items themselves, and the stories surrounding them, to really think about my grandmother as a person other than "Grandma."

We were cuddled on the sofa in my parent's knotty wood-paneled 1970s style den, and I remember asking, "Grandma, what was your job for Mrs. Roskin?" She leaned in, confiding, "Oh, Kelley, I did everything for her, handled all of her affairs. But most importantly, I was her confidante, her trusted advisor, and her most steadfast friend."

I nodded, fascinated as always by the dramatic language and passion my grandmother brought to every conversation. It didn't really occur to me in that moment that this was a rather unorthodox job description. I just drank it all in: my grandmother, the trusted advisor.

Later, after Grandma and Grandpa had driven back to New York in their cavernous Oldsmobile (Grandma buttoned stylishly into her "car coat" in the passenger seat), I proudly showed my mother the sparkling evening purse. I was chattering on about how exciting Grandma's life and jobs in New York had been when I glimpsed a fleeting sadness in my mother's eyes. "Kelley," she said quietly, "Grandma was Mrs. Roskin's maid."

At the time, my teenage self was a bit let down. My glamorous grandma from New York was a maid? But now, her life and legacy is something I am fiercely proud of. The optimistic and passionate way my grandmother lived her life taught me a valuable lesson: that the situation you find yourself in, whether it's your job or your health or your family, does not define who you are. Our essential spirit does not have to reflect our external circumstance.

I have no doubt that my grandmother, who worked for Mrs. Roskin for more than thirty years, did become her trusted advisor, her true and constant friend. My grandmother worked hard, did her job with extraordinary care and pride, and thrived in her adopted America. The spirit of my grandmother, and those like her, is the spirit that has made this country great.

Julia O'Toole Wessell took great satisfaction in the fact that she was a hard worker who helped support her family of four children through very difficult times. Yes, she loved glamour and elegance, and yes, she was a maid. She saw no disconnect in that. And thanks to her, neither do I. The value of doing a job and doing it well is enough in itself.

Anthony Trollope wrote that while it is necessary for a young person

KC

"*You must learn some of my philosophy.*
*Think only of the past as its remembrance gives you pleasure.*"

Jane Austen, *Pride and Prejudice*

starting out in life to decide whether he will make hats or shoes, the more important decision is whether to make excellent—or mediocre—hats or shoes. My grandmother cleaned, tidied, organized, and beautified. She did her job with excellence, and she did it with inimitable style.

I know some people might say my grandmother was an embellisher, someone who made her life out to be something it really wasn't. I disagree. She had the ability to take whatever she had, no matter how small, and truly make it shine. There was something utterly compelling and undeniably American about her optimism. She never felt sorry for herself. She put on her lipstick—usually a bright Max Factor coral—fixed a nice pot of tea and had a good laugh.

She adored looking good. My grandmother was one of those women who never gave up on the idea of herself as a desirable, beautiful woman. Just coming over for dinner with our family, when she was well into her eighties, Grandma would be fully made up, hair styled, wearing a great outfit and jewelry. She was quite censorious of the sweat suit wearers of our time. She believed in making an effort.

This outlook was forged over decades of living a life that was never easy. As I grew older, my mother told me more stories of how she and her two sisters and brother worked all through school to help keep their struggling family afloat. My grandfather, Harry Wessell, a first generation American, worked construction and helped build the Holland Tunnel. His father, Thor Albert Wessell, had come through Ellis Island from Sweden in 1890.

My grandfather grew up in the gritty Hell's Kitchen section of Manhattan, home to many poor and working class immigrants at the time. He had to quit school in the eighth grade to help put food on the table. Like my grandmother, he was a dreamer and an optimist. He tried to start several businesses but was usually unsuccessful. Despite his lack of education, he was a prolific writer of fiery letters to the editor of the local newspapers throughout his life.

My mother and all of her siblings worked various jobs after school from an early age to help support their family. My mom, a pretty, popular majorette in high school, worked in the cafeteria, cleaning trays and wiping down tables between lunch shifts to get the hot lunch for free.

I asked her once if she was ever embarrassed about cleaning the cafeteria in front of her friends and I was surprised by her response: "No!" she said. "I was really proud of myself for getting that job, which lots of other kids wanted back then. I earned the money to buy myself a hot lunch, which was great since I was sick of packing peanut butter sandwiches." By today's standards, they were poor, but my mother doesn't ever remember feeling that way. She believes my grandparents' outlook, their optimism and humor, fierce pride and work ethic, had everything to do with that, in spite of the hard times.

My mother remembers the year that my grandfather lost all of their savings in a failed construction venture and couldn't find work. My mother, her older sister, and brother had outgrown their coats and had nothing to get them though the freezing upstate New York winter. The family had only one car and everyone had to do lots of walking, no matter the weather.

During that difficult season, my grandparents gratefully accepted

coats and clothing from the Salvation Army, whose kind volunteers also showed up at their door with a Christmas dinner, complete with a small, brightly decorated bottle brush tree and wrapped toys. My Aunt Julie still remembers how delighted she was with her gift, a soft brown teddy bear.

According to my mother, accepting this charity hurt my grandparents' pride, but there was no other choice. They survived the winter, but my grandmother never forgot how humbling it was to be the recipient of those donated coats and gifts. The following year, the day after Thanksgiving, my grandmother woke my mother and her older sister early and took them down to the Salvation Army to ring the bell and help out.

My mother told me that she only once dared to complain about having to get up early to volunteer for the Salvation Army. "My mother set me straight," she said. "She looked me hard in the eye and said, 'We have a debt to the Salvation Army. They gave us Christian charity when we needed them. And we will repay our debt by helping them help others. We will hold our heads high.'"

This was the pride of my grandmother, and the work ethic of her entire generation. You could not hold your head high without hard work. They may have received coats from the Salvation Army one year, but they would help give them out the next.

In spite of these hardships, my grandmother had a great hopefulness about her that never wavered. Many immigrants of her generation expected life to be hard and full of struggle, so they kept their dreams modest, their lives focused on saving and preparing themselves for whatever loss or difficulty lay around the corner.

But my grandmother, even into her old age, kept a joyful expectation of surprise about her. I know her strong faith in God's goodness was a big part of that. She always had a beautiful strand of rosary beads nearby that I found fascinating and mysterious, having been raised a Baptist. Her Catholic faith was an integral part of her inherent optimism, a source of both joy and sustenance for her.

She and my grandfather did achieve their own piece of the American dream. All four of their children were successful and helped them in their own ways after my grandparents retired. My grandparents eventually left New York and settled into a small rented house near my parents' home in Russellville, Kentucky, where Grandma was an immediate hit, charming everyone in town with her infectious laughter and irresistible tales. In the winters, they enjoyed a month at my parents' beachfront condo in Florida, playing golf and making friends with the other retired snowbirds.

With her musical Irish brogue, stylish scarves, and love of a highball by the pool, I'll bet those other retired ladies had no idea just how hard my grandmother's life had been. Not that she would want them to— she would much rather brag about her successful, educated children and grandchildren, her American dream.

She always made me feel that I had made her proud, and she absolutely adored Rand. He used to joke that Grandma was good for his ophthalmology practice. Whenever she had an appointment to see him, she would sit in the waiting room and brag to anyone within earshot about what a brilliant surgeon he was. "He knows everything about the eye, don't you know," she would say in serious, confiding tones to whomever was seated next to her.

She was that way with all of her children and grandchildren: lavish with praise, delighted with even the smallest achievement, and a true believer in all of our best qualities and talents. I remember taking her to Wal-Mart when I was home for a visit from college, and she walked me around the store so she could introduce me to the manager and all of her favorite cashiers, just so they could see "how gorgeous my granddaughter is!" While it was occasionally embarrassing, she made each of us feel special, worthy, and loved.

## In Memory

The last time that I saw my grandmother was in July of 1996. I'll never forget that afternoon, and it has served as a reminder to me ever since—a reminder to recognize what is truly important in life, even in the busyness of the everyday, and make time for it and value it.

It was around three in the afternoon and I had just gotten our four-month-old baby Duncan down for a nap. I had sent three-year-old William off to the park with a babysitter while I hastily readied my house for cookout guests that evening. I was fairly new to both cooking and entertaining and not feeling at all confident as I rushed around picking up toy trucks, cleaning surfaces, marinating chicken, and chopping vegetables.

I was panicking a bit and starting to regret inviting so many people. I impatiently barked hello into the phone when it wouldn't stop ringing. It was my mother. "Hey honey!" she said. "I brought Grandma over to Bowling Green and we just got out of her doctor's appointment. She feels a little more energetic today and wants to stop by your house for a quick visit."

My first reaction, I'm ashamed to say, was annoyance. Didn't my mom remember I was hosting a cookout for my new book club and their spouses tonight? I was way behind on my food prep and needed to sweep the deck and wipe at least half the fingerprints from the glass doors before my guests arrived. My boys had consumed all of my energy that morning and I hadn't even had a shower yet. I most certainly did not have time to sit and chat with Mom and Grandma.

I opened my mouth to start my excuses but something in my mother's voice stopped me cold. Grandma had been losing weight and I knew my mom was worried about her. I found myself saying, "Sure, come on over. I'm here." In the fifteen minutes before they arrived I kicked about a hundred Legos and Thomas Trains under the couch, dramatically lowered my standards for the presentation of my home, and put my hair in a ponytail.

We sat on the deck in the light summer sunshine. I brought Grandma a glass of white wine. We talked and laughed. Listening to the rainfall of her words, I remember feeling an unusual lack of concern about the ticking clock, the impending arrival of my guests, my messy house and unprepared meal. The afternoon sun felt good as I relaxed and enjoyed the unexpected time with her and my mom. It wasn't often that it was just the three of us anymore.

Grandma finished her wine and said she was getting tired. I told her that I was so glad that she had made the impromptu visit, and I meant it. She looked out at the backyard of my new home, with its towering oak and hickory trees and view of the lake. She smiled and said, "Everything is so lovely here, Kelley. I always knew you would have such a beautiful home. I know you are going to have much happiness here, and you deserve it, my love." And she smiled with her shining blue eyes. It felt like a benediction. My happiness was hers. That is what it means to be a mother, a grandmother, to love someone more than yourself. It was a diaphanous moment, pure and light.

My grandmother died suddenly the next night. I am forever grateful for that final, golden afternoon with her and my mother.

Fifteen years later, I carried Grandma's castoff purse to the White House Christmas Party. As I walked into the foyer, my eyes were wide with the beauty and grandeur of it all—the dozens of sparkling Christmas trees, the Marine Band in their gleaming red and gold brocade uniforms, the glittering people standing in those historic marble halls filled with paintings and crystal chandeliers. Standing there, I took a deep breath and looked down at my arm. That little beaded purse just shined. And I knew Grandma was smiling.

JoAnn Abdelwahabe

# chapter three

# Courage

> *"Don't wish me happiness.*
> *I don't expect to be happy all the time.*
> *It has gotten beyond that somehow.*
> *Wish me courage, and strength, and*
> *a sense of humor. I will need them all."*
> Anne Morrow Lindbergh
> *A Gift from the Sea*

# Salvaged Heirlooms
# from Faraway Places

*"Bir elin nesi var, Iki elin sesi var."*
*"One hand has nothing, two hands have sound."*

Turkish saying, author unknown

There is a certain power in old things that are loved and handed down, carrying their stories with them like a message in a bottle. My friend Sevgi built a business by taking very old, worn-out things, Turkish kilim rugs, and transforming them into beautiful, purposeful things—unique purses and bags, shoes, belts and other accessories.

She called her business Carpetbackers. She scoured the bazaars and second-hand shops of Turkey for her rugs, created designs for her factory there, and sold them at wholesale markets all over the United States. I have one of her purses and I love the artistry and intricacy of the kilim rug design, but also the idea that long ago in a distant country this was part of someone's home, someone's life, was lived on and worn out—and then recreated into something stylish and beautiful that is sporting about the US in 2015.

Sevgi and I used to marvel at the coincidence that we became friends at a small liberal arts college in Memphis, Tennessee, in 1981, after we had both lived in Turkey as children at the same time during the early seventies. She lived in Istanbul and I lived in Izmir, but we traveled to each other's cities quite often, and I like to think that we passed each other in a bazaar or marketplace back then, smiling shyly as we picked out trinkets or sweets from a street vendor's cart.

My father was an Air Force Sergeant and our family moved around the world for much of my childhood. My parents and brothers lived in England before I came along in September of 1963, at Homestead Air Force Base near Miami. I started kindergarten at General Arnold School in Lincoln Nebraska, but before that I had already lived in Myrtle Beach, South Carolina and Austin, Texas – a true Air Force brat.

When I was in second grade my Dad got the news that we would be transferred to Izmir, Turkey. Turkey? We were all anxious about it, having no idea what to expect from life in a Muslim country so exotic and far away, but our two years there became my family's most memorable, wonderful adventure.

I loved everything about Turkey—the beautiful, dramatic beaches and landscape, the language, the colorful, chaotic bazaars, the friendly people and outlandish street peddlers to whom my mother would call down from our apartment balcony for chai in the afternoons. Wiry brown boys would carry it up on elaborate brass trays, the hot chai steaming in its tiny, exquisite gold-rimmed glasses.

Every week my mother would send me flying down the stairs with a few liras to buy Turkish sweets and candies from the cart vendors, yelling out in my meager Turkish, *"Geliyorum!"* (Hold on, I'm coming!). The peddlers always had a big smile for the small American girl with the wispy white-blonde hair and the sweet tooth.

I immediately became friends with a little Turkish girl in our building, the apartment manager's daughter, and I would often have dinner with their family, seated on richly colored kilim rugs on the floor. Their doorway was covered with beautiful blue glass "evil eyes" to ward off bad spirits, and I was mesmerized by it. None of them spoke a word of English and I spoke no Turkish in the beginning, but that did not get in our way— we were both seven-year-old girls who loved dolls, and that was all that mattered.

My new friend was fascinated with my extensive collection of Barbies and their stylish American wardrobes and accessories. She and I would play for hours, sending Barbie, PJ, and Skipper out on all kinds of perfectly accessorized adventures speaking "half-half" Turkish-English. I can still see my Malibu Barbie, coolly insouciant as she lounged on exotic kilim rug beaches in her bikini and tiny sunglasses.

I certainly didn't expect to meet my next Turkish friend in 1981 in Memphis, Tennessee, but I'm so very grateful that I did. Sevgi is one of the bravest, most unconventional people I have ever met. She never takes the expected path, but instead forges ahead with something no one else has thought of. She was a Phi Beta Kappa business major, but instead of taking an entry-level job somewhere in Atlanta with the rest of us after college, she signed with a modeling agency and flew off to Japan to work. (Yes, she's tall and beautiful too.)

A few years later she started her business, managing production from her factory in Turkey and traveling across the US to merchandise her products. Fluent in four languages, Sevgi has lived all over the world and recently returned full time to the United States after living in Gibraltar for eight years.

When I think of Sevgi, I am reminded of these words from Helen Keller: *Life is either a daring adventure or nothing at all.* Sevgi's story is about two women, Bedia and Sumer, her grandmother and mother, both of whom personify a true sense of daring, adventure, and love of life.

> *"I was no longer scared.*
> *I could see what was inside me."*
> Amy Tan
> *The Joy Luck Club*

# Turkish Rebels
## Sevgi's Story

My mother Sumer was just one year old when it happened, too young to comprehend the incident that caused her mother to develop a hard, impenetrable shell, withholding the love and warmth that she so desperately needed. As my grandmother Bedia was changing her diaper one morning, Kaya, her firstborn son, who had been playing by her side just seconds before, was suddenly nowhere in sight. In terror, Bedia stared at the wind-ruffled curtains of the open fifth-floor window.

The day before, Kaya had been mesmerized by an acrobat walking on a tightrope. Maneuvering his tiny body through the window guards, Kaya was seen by neighbors trying to balance himself on the ledge, holding out his arms, shouting, "Look at me! Look at me!" Down the steps ran my desperate grandmother. Grabbing her son, she ran all the way to the hospital ten blocks away, clutching his lifeless body.

Sumer's childhood was infused with the feeling that her mother was withdrawn from her, unlike the way she treated her older sister and brothers. "She doesn't like me," Sumer told her older sister when she was five years old. In horror, she listened to her sister explain what had happened four years earlier. From that day on, feeling forlorn and responsible, she recoiled from her distant mother, the wall between the two growing taller.

Sumer grew up in an old neighborhood in Istanbul, with cobblestone streets and slanted wooden buildings. Bedia, who was fiercely feminist, shunned wearing a veil and refused to set foot in a mosque, where women and men had to pray separately. She was tough, having worked in a factory at the age of ten while her father was at war and her mother pregnant.

When my grandfather, Arif, was stricken with severe diabetes and had to quit his job, Bedia took control and started working from home sewing scarves for Vakko Department Store. All day she toiled in front of the sewing machine, a filterless Birinci cigarette hanging from her mouth. In the evenings, she liked to play solitaire as Arif read *Pardayanlar*, a swashbuckler series, to the children and their friends. The diabetes did little to thwart his humor—my mother remembers his laughter permeating the house.

Forced to grow up at a tender age, Sumer's shyness and insecurity gave way to a strong and independent spirit. She adored school. "Raise your hand if you have a piano at home and would like to take piano lessons at lunchtime," asked the teacher one day. Sumer's hand was the first to go up.

"Your daughter is a very talented piano player," the teacher told her mother at a school meeting months later. Bedia was taken aback. "But we have no piano at home," she answered. That evening, with her head held low, Sumer led her mother to the windowsill where she had hand-drawn a keyboard, hidden safely behind the curtains. A few days later, Sumer came home to find two men hauling a piano up the staircase.

Sumer and her sister had to eventually quit school to stay at home sewing scarves to help make ends meet. When old enough, they both began work as "coffee girls" at the Istanbul Hilton Hotel, wearing ornate Turkish costumes, and befriending travelers from all over the world. One such group was the Copp family of Memphis, Tennessee, who asked her if she would like to be sponsored and return to the United States with them.

"No," her parents told her, "absolutely not!" Persistent and determined, Sumer sought the help of an influential friend, a well-known Turkish poet, and was able to access the necessary paperwork for her move to the United States, only to defiantly inform her parents the night before her departure.

In Memphis, living in the posh yet warm home of the Copp family in

Morningside Park, Sumer attended White Station High School. With just six years of education behind her, she tested at the senior level after one year at White Station.

A newspaper article about her in the *Memphis Commercial Appeal* prompted The Lausanne School for Girls to offer her a full scholarship for her senior year. While studying at Lausanne, Sumer became a scholarship student at Memphis College of Music. After graduation, she was awarded a full scholarship to study voice at what is now Rhodes College, where I would attend decades later.

Through friends there, she met and fell in love with my father. With her dreams set on studying opera at Juilliard, she discovered she was pregnant with my sister. Marriage and three more children quickly followed. The "Turkish Girl" at first felt unaccepted by my father's traditional southern family, but she soon captured their hearts with her warmth and beauty.

They settled in Memphis and my father began working alongside his dad in the appliance parts business started by my entrepreneurial grandfather. It was Memphis in the early sixties: a hotbed of racial tension and social change. Just like her mother Bedia, who had rebelled against the second-class treatment of women in religion, Sumer's sense of justice and defiant spirit led her straight into the Civil Rights Movement.

In her Volkswagen Kombi, Sumer drove black voters to and from the voting booths. She opened a bank account at Tri-State Bank, which had mostly black customers, where she made many friends. Supporters and friends of Dr. Martin Luther King, Jr., such as Dr. Billy Kyles, frequented our home, where my mother and father hosted social gatherings and meetings.

When Dr. King arrived in Memphis for a televised church service, Sumer was the only white person sitting in the choir pews. During the service, when all stood up, hand in hand, singing "We Shall Overcome," Dr King, who had been sitting in front of my mother, turned around and noticed her. The cameras zoomed in as he leaned over to embrace her, and they finished the song with their hands clasped.

When my parents returned home that night, they found my irate great-grandfather, who was unaccepting of their involvement in the Civil

Rights Movement, waiting for them at the front door. I can only imagine the shouting match that ensued, but my parents were unyielding. Together they forged their own social circles in Memphis, raising their young family with values of social justice and respect.

In 1967, eleven years after leaving Turkey, Sumer returned home for a visit. Old friends, who had heard of her American training in voice and piano, encouraged her to perform at a local festival. The crowd was mesmerized by her operatic vibrato as she sang popular American songs like "Summertime" and Elvis Presley's "In the Ghetto." The audiences grew larger and more enthusiastic as she performed several more times during her visit.

Sumer's dreams of singing and performing were reignited, and with four children in tow, my parents moved from Memphis to Istanbul. My father found work as a contractor providing goods for the PX stores, where military personnel in Turkey shopped for US products. He loved his new life in Turkey, where he charmed everyone he met with his friendly manner and captivating blue eyes. My mother was quickly on her way to becoming a famous pop singer, performing in concerts across the country and releasing the first of several albums. Then, in May of 1970, our world came crashing down when my father was killed in a car accident. He was 35.

My mother was devastated. With four children to support, she went into survival mode and continued her singing career. Performing regularly at a club nearby, she managed to keep us all going on her own. There was nothing she couldn't do. I remember how she rolled up her sleeves at home, even fixing the heating unit in our house herself, her slender arms covered in black soot.

For extra income, our beautifully renovated two-story home in Tarabya, a suburb of Istanbul, was turned into a makeshift movie set for Turkish films. Tall light fixtures were constantly carried up and down the stairs, the floors and furniture meticulously wiped and polished for each scene. With the income from the movie business and her singing, my mother was able to provide us with a beautiful home with a large garden filled with fruit trees and a swing set that still sits there today.

We regularly spent time with my grandmother Bedia and grandfather Arif, and also my mother's siblings. I remember my grandfather Arif making us laugh with his stories as we four grandchildren stood in line to massage his achy shoulders in exchange for fruit candies and liras. I remember my grandmother Bedia as a tough woman with a work-hardened face who would suddenly surprise me with a fierce bear hug.

My mother says she will never forget the look of shock and pride in Bedia's eyes the first time she saw her sing onstage. She was overcome with joy that Sumer had accomplished something that she herself was never allowed. It was only then that Sumer learned that Bedia had also once dreamed of being a singer, had even sung on one of the very first records ever produced in Turkey in 1936, but her disapproving family considered it scandalous and stopped the release of the record.

Sumer still struggled with the wall that existed between her and her mother, but sensed that Bedia was proud of all she had accomplished in the years since her defiant act of running away to the United States in high school. In 1972, Bedia was diagnosed with liver cancer. Ironically, my mother was the only sibling at her side in her last moments.

As she held her mother in the hospital bed, Bedia's protective shield broke away and she tearfully apologized for holding back the love she felt she could not relinquish for all those years. When her soul left her body, Bedia's hardened, lined features finally softened and became a face at peace, the look of a woman reunited with her three-year-old son.

Suffering this second loss, my mother courageously carried on. She gave us a childhood of music and laughter, despite her own pain. She threw her energy into her career, recording several more albums. She became a famous pop star, and we four children even performed on one of her albums, singing the Turkish version of "Sing a Song" by The Carpenters.

Television appearances followed, and soon the paparazzi began to intrude on our lives. Alone, my mother felt unable to protect us from a stalker who eventually set fire to the utility room adjacent to our house. After that, the demands of her celebrity and career on the heels of so much loss became overwhelming and she decided to move us back to Memphis in January of 1975, where our American grandparents welcomed us home with open arms.

I was twelve years old. Although we had spent several summers in the United States with my grandparents, moving back was a culture shock. Television and toys replaced climbing trees, playing soccer, jumping into the Bosphorus with our dogs, picking fruit, and growing vegetable gardens. School was now "too easy," and it took some time before friendships formed. At first we did not fit in and had to survive the persistent teasing refrain, "Turkey…Gobble! Gobble!"

Our return coincided with the start of busing, which my mother celebrated despite the heated resistance of many during that time. Some transferred to private schools, but Sumer was determined that we remain in the public system. Her dream of seeing her children receive a top-quality music education was fulfilled, as we all excelled in our school band program.

With her outgoing personality, my mother became a confidant of many of our friends, and our home the neighborhood hangout. Not only was she doing the job of double-parenting four kids, she was becoming, as we grew older, our best friend.

As we all left home to attend college and tackle life, my mother found an opportunity to return to Turkey in 1987 and has been living there ever since. Sadly, the country has taken a terrible turn in recent years, with increasingly less religious and social tolerance. My mother described it to me eloquently in a letter:

> "It is a recurring nightmare from which one cannot break free. The sun is shining with total absence of light—garlands of ignorance, greed, wickedness, deception, chicanery, cruelty; vultures in turbans and brides in black veils—spiraling undercurrent gobbling up all that is good—art, music, ballet, theater, poetry, philosophy, and basic freedom. Women are sent back to the Middle Ages and little boys are being brainwashed. Bleak? Oh, yes. Worst of all? No one in the world cares."

It is a sad irony that my passionate and adventurous mother, who has bravely stood up for justice throughout her life and taken great risks to fulfill her dreams, is now watching her beloved homeland become less free and tolerant than it was more than forty years ago. In her seventies now, she remains defiant. She stands, a testament to all that can be accomplished by a woman of fortitude and daring, unafraid to venture beyond the safe and comfortable confines created by others. Her name is Sumer. She stands.

# chapter four

# Friendship

"Nobody sees a flower really; it is so small.
We haven't time, and to see takes time —
Like to have a friend takes time."

Georgia O'Keeffe

# Taking a Chance
# and Making a Friend

People who are optimistic take more chances, and the more chances you take, the more good things happen. Like most people, I would say the best things in my life have happened when I put myself out there and made myself a little vulnerable. That's how I met my friend Brigid.

At seventeen, my parents let me fly alone to Memphis, Tennessee to attend a prospective student weekend at Rhodes College. I was beyond excited. I showed up in Memphis wearing a navy blazer, gold add-a-bead necklace, monogrammed crew neck sweater, madras plaid pants, Bass Weejuns, and one of those monogrammed purses with the interchangeable covers you could match with your outfit. I had even color-coordinated the striped grosgrain band on my tank watch. It was 1981 and *The Preppy Handbook* was my style bible. I was determined to land in Memphis *not* looking like who I really was—a small girl from a small town, eager but secretly scared.

When I arrived at Rhodes, I was awestruck by the beauty of the campus. Its gorgeous stone buildings, gothic towers, and oak-lined lawns were a postcard of what college should look like. Watching all the fresh-faced students as they laughed and talked on their way to class, I knew immediately that I wanted to fit right in.

At the check-in desk, a counselor gave me an information folder and introduced me to the student host I would be staying with, waving over a girl with waist length hair, a flowy, bohemian dress, and some kind of half-combat boot, half-fisherman sandal on her feet. She had painted her fingernails matte black.

Around me swirled the sorority girls and their prospective students, laughing and making plans to attend the football tailgate the next afternoon. My student host was kind and polite and, looking back, more indulgent of my over-the-top outfit than I was of hers, but I was disappointed.

She lived in the foreign-language dorm. Her room was filled with plants, guitars, and hand-thrown pottery. She was an art major who spoke several languages. I met her roommate, who played the harp, and a few other girls, none of whom knew or cared anything about the football tailgate or the fraternity parties going on that night. Two of them were conversing in Italian. In a few years, my twenty-year-old self would know that these girls were very cool, but my seventeen-year-old, plaid-pant-wearing self was desperate to get out of there and meet the Chi Omegas, Tri Deltas, and cute SAEs.

When she dropped me off in the main hall for the Prospective Student information session, I looked longingly at the other girls, who all seemed to be ensconced in lively, chatty groups of twos and threes. I felt lonely and, worse than that, embarrassed to be alone, the way you do in large crowds, especially at seventeen.

I sat miserably for a while, until I realized the only way I was going to have someone to talk to would be to make the first move and actually talk to someone. I forced a smile and broke into the conversation to my right. At first the girls were aloof, but the one next to me was actually quite friendly once the ice was broken. We whispered through the boring Dean of Students' lecture, but once it was over, she picked up her sweater and turned to leave with her friend. "Nice to meet you!" she trilled over her shoulder. My heart sank.

"Umm… what are y'all doing for dinner?" I asked, humiliated to be so pushy but also fiercely determined not to go back to the Foreign Language Dorm for the evening harp concert. "We have plans with our boyfriends," the not-so-nice one said briskly. (They had boyfriends here already? My humiliation was complete!)

But the girl I had so determinedly chatted with took pity on me. "Yes, we're meeting them right now," she said. "But there are a bunch of girls here from Little Rock back in our dorm. I got to know one of them, Brigid, this morning. She's really fun. I think they're going out to dinner at Overton Square. If you want to follow us back to the dorm, I'll introduce you." I grabbed this lifeline with both hands and trailed behind them like an unwanted puppy, eager to meet these "fun" girls and hoping they would let me tag along.

And that's how I met Brigid. The introduction was ignominious, to say the least. My other new "friend" was painfully obvious in her eagerness to dump me and get on with her evening. She literally pushed me forward, saying flatly, "This is Kelley. She doesn't have anyone to go out with tonight. Can she go with you guys?" I was mortified, feeling like the oddball cousin your mom insists be "included."

Brigid, confident looking and beautiful with her big dark eyes, had been laughing with all her friends from Little Rock until I was abruptly foisted on her. They all went quiet as I was appraised. Brigid paused an agonizing second or two, clearly trying to think of a polite rejection since I was so ridiculously prepped out (they were all rather more restrained in their use of madras and monograms), but then she smiled and gave me a rather unsure, "Sure!" I was swamped with relief. I knew they would like me if they gave me a chance!

I had a ball that night. Brigid was cool and irreverent without being pretentious or snobby, and I liked her immediately. She regaled me with funny stories of her horrible ex-boyfriend and summer job at Godfather's Pizza. We both loved to read, planned to major in English, and were obsessed with The Go-Go's and The Police. (Brigid would start a new wave band, Brigid and the Neutrons, our freshman year. Margaret and I were her backup singers—although I have some suspicion that my mic was turned off after the first rehearsal.)

We couldn't wait to start our big college adventure, filled not just with the obligatory great learning and preparation for exciting, high paying careers, but lots of parties with all the cute boys roaming that campus. For

KC

me, college began that night, even though its official start was nearly nine months away. I had made the first move, and it was awkward and embarrassing, like a lot of first steps, but it was worth it. I had made a friend. Is there anything sweeter?

Brigid once wrote me a letter that she closed with the sentence, "Thank you, my true and constant friend." It made me feel deeply happy to know that I had been that to her, and I have never forgotten those beautiful words.

Brigid is my free spirit friend, a dreamer and a seeker. Raised in a staunch Catholic household, she is now a practicing Buddhist, and writes a thoughtful, funny, wonderful blog called, "Adventures of a Southern Buddhist Catholic." Her spirituality has always reminded me of this quote from one of my favorite books from my college days, Walker Percy's *The Moviegoer:*

*"What do you seek—God? You ask with a smile. I hesitate to answer, since all other Americans have settled the matter for themselves and to give such an answer would amount to setting myself a goal which everyone else has reached—and therefore raising a question in which no one has the slightest interest. Who wants to be dead last among one hundred and eighty million Americans? For, as everyone knows, the polls report that 98% of Americans believe in God and the remaining 2% are atheists and agnostics – which leaves not a single percentage point for a seeker."*

Like me, Brigid was an English major at Rhodes. She has made a career as a writer and editor, and was Director of Advertising at Turner Network Television before walking away from the corporate world and driving alone to Mexico in her ancient BMW 320i, in order to devote herself fully to writing and contemplating her next life move.

We are an odd match in a way. I am more conservative and risk-averse by nature (some would say conventional!) and I worried about her during that time. She came away from that experience knowing that she no longer wanted to work for a big corporate entity—that she wanted, as she writes on her blog, "to focus on words, and living a happy life."

When I asked my friends to tell me personal stories of the women in their lives for this book, I was disappointed when Brigid didn't share one at our reunion. She later admitted to me that she was daunted by the request, which surprised me as she makes her living as a freelance writer. "I listened to the stories and memories you each shared," she said, "and I felt sad and regretful that I had never really connected with my mother or a grandmother the way so many of you have."

A few weeks later she sent me the beautiful essay on the following page. "I'm grateful now that you came up with this idea," she wrote, "because it really helped me to examine and come to terms with so much about my mother and our relationship." Her story, "Are You My Mother?" reveals that we don't always understand life's lessons while we are learning them, and that one of the great blessings of time is the ability to see with older eyes.

# Are You My Mother?
## Brigid's Story

One warm summer morning after my mother left for work, I slipped into her bedroom and opened the bottom drawer of her dresser. Carefully pushing aside the garter belt and girdle and silk stockings, I foraged for a book entitled, *Am I Becoming A Woman?* I was ten years old and although I didn't understand what was inside the pages of that book, I had a feeling it contained secrets that I needed to know. I caught a glimpse of its cover once when I borrowed my Mom's brocade purse to play dress up. She kept the lovely evening bag wrapped in plastic in that drawer. With its little gold clasp and a gold chain handle, its very presence fascinated me. When did my practical mother ever have use for such a thing? Not once had I seen her put on garters and silk stockings and carry her little evening bag out for a night on the town.

Beneath the purse was the book but there was also another plastic bag. This one contained four birth certificates. Mine was on the top. My name was spelled in calligraphy: Bridget. Not Brigid, which is how I always spelled my name. Odd. I read on and saw that my mother was forty-three when I was born. Since I was ten, that would make her fifty-three, ancient by my reckoning. I never thought of my mother as an age before then, but afterward I noticed that she'd say things such as, "I don't like how my legs look in shorts," or "Don't take my photo now, I'm not wearing makeup." At the time I thought she was just being silly. I thought my mother was beautiful. I didn't care if she had spidery varicose veins. I just wanted her to come swimming with me. I didn't see the lines that time scribed into her face. I only wanted her to sit with me and tell me stories. Now, as I find myself nearing the same age, I realize what she meant—and it makes me sad that I didn't know her.

I never really knew my mother. At least I didn't know much about her. She was a quiet woman who didn't speak of her past. And yet, I know she had another life, long before I was born.

Mom attended Saint Anthony's School of Nursing in Oklahoma City from 1944 to 1948. She received her RN and worked in the operating room. I know this because she sometimes spoke of her time in surgery, which amazed me that my gentle mother could withstand the sight of blood and gore. After she passed away, I found a box she kept in her closet filled with small 2" x 4" black-and-white photos, a collection of funny, old postcards and letters from her mother, my grandmother, who died when I was just three years old.

The little black-and-white photos provided clues about who my mother once was. In these images a young woman smoked cigarettes, traveled to New York City with her girlfriends, studied on her twin bed in a dorm room and wore fashionable suits with shoulder pads as thick and sturdy as a linebacker's, her lips painted slick and red.

There are dozens of images of Mom with her best friend Margaret Ann Brown and other girls identified as Diane, Isabel, Loretta and Rita. Their names are scrawled in my mother's scratchy script on the backs of some of these images. They are smiling girls who pose in modest swimsuits, stylish dresses, and starched white nursing uniforms, complete with black capes. And there's Mom's graduation portrait, depicting a beautiful young woman with perfect, smooth skin and deep brown eyes, dark as onyx marbles. Her face was fuller and rounder than I recall, her dark curls to her shoulders and her smart nursing cap affixed like a halo above her head.

Was she as virtuous as she appeared? She was attractive and—judging by the photos— outgoing and friendly, so surely she must have had beaus before

Brown 'me' Loretta Rita

she met my Dad in 1949. But to hear her tell the tale, "There was no one special." I suspect that No One Special broke her heart along the way. If so, she never gave him a name.

In another box on the shelf were letters about Nick, my mother's twin brother who disappeared in World War II. He was an airplane mechanic in the Army Air Corps, assigned to cargo planes flying over The Hump across the high, Himalayan Mountains. At the end of the war, his plane crashed and neither it nor the crew were ever found. Letters and copies of letters from Nick before he disappeared, telegrams from the War Department, and sepia news clippings about other similar incidents were tucked away in that box.

From time to time, one of my sisters or I would become curious and retrieve the box from the closet and go through it as though it were a puzzle filled with jigsaw pieces. We would empty out the contents and sift through the clues. We thought if we pondered over the evidence long enough, a clear picture might form of what happened to the uncle we never knew.

I believe my mother held out hope throughout her life that he was still alive. "I still just can't believe it," she told me one night as we drove home from a family gathering. "I still can't believe he's gone." The war had taken its toll on her; it extracted a great price.

I never knew my mother. I wove her legend from expressions in black-and-white photos, from her quiet responses and from scraps of history tucked away in cardboard boxes kept high on her closet shelves. I stitched her story together from scraps that fell from her lips on rare occasions when she spoke of the life she led before she became my Mom.

As I entered puberty, our relationship began to stretch thin in the typical tug-of-war between mothers who want to protect and daughters who want to be free. But we found a common ground in fashion. Although most of my wardrobe came from J.C. Penney or Sears or my sisters' hand-me-downs, sometimes I'd wander into M.M. Cohn, the upscale department store in town, and find a dress or skirt I liked.

Sometimes my mother would assess the garment and its price tag and whisper, "We can make that for so much less," as if the clerk might overhear our scheme to copy the design.

Then she'd send me to the dressing room to try on the coveted item. She'd fish out a deposit slip or grocery receipt and a pencil from her purse and sketch the garment as I modeled it, turning this way and that before the three-way mirror, admiring the cut of the skirt or the softness of the chintz.

"Stand still so I can see how it's made!" she'd say.

I would wait for her to finish her assessment. Then we'd retreat to Hancock's fabric store to find the necessary items.

My favorite time with Mom was spent inhaling the starchy perfume in the rows of fabric bolts. Perched on a hard stool near the front of the store, I poured over pattern catalogs until I found a Simplicity design that was close in style to the dress I coveted. Mom would peer over my shoulder and nod, or suggest a modification or two.

Late in the evenings, after dinner dishes were left drying beside the sink and crumbs had been swept from the floor, my job was to carefully cut out the tissue paper pattern. Spreading the fabric out on the floor, Mom knelt and pinned the thin, brown papers onto the cloth. While she pinned and cut, I sat nearby running my fingers through the collections of buttons she kept in an old oatmeal canister. Nothing went to waste.

I tried my hand at sewing in a high school home economics class but found the work tedious and confusing. Although I managed to stitch together an A-line skirt, most of my projects ended up in my mother's scrap bag.

As I edged toward college, our differences became more apparent—or so I felt. By this time Mom was sixty-one and I was eighteen and the gap between us widened, but we still came together over patterns and fabric and notions as she sewed up the prom dresses I designed. My senior year, I wanted a sexy, strapless green velvet gown with a straight skirt and a slit up the side to my thigh, and she created it. Tailor-made and of my design, it was a perfect fit. But I wonder now how she felt as I primped before the mirror, tugging up the bodice to hide what little cleavage I had and smoothing the velvet skirt over my hips. She let me go to the dance that night wearing that sexy dress and four-inch heels and too much eye makeup. She never did talk to me about sex. I suppose she thought I'd figured it out by that time. But I hadn't. Not really.

I wanted my mother to be someone she wasn't. I wanted a TV sit-com mom like the ones on the shows I watched every week. I wanted a mom who could sit lightly on the corner of my flower-power comforter, smooth my soft, blonde hair (I'm a brunette), listen intently to my sorrows, and find the exact, scripted words to soothe all my insecurities and make me feel good. My self-centered teenage heart could not see that Mom conveyed her love by the late-night hum of her sewing machine.

I wanted a mother who would be my conspirator. I wanted a mother who could teach me what it meant to be sexy and strong. And last but not least, I needed a role model to help me understand what it meant to be a mother when my turn came along. I received it all.

Were there days when my mother looked at me and wondered who I was? Or did she recognize herself in me? Did I inherit her longing for better things in life? Did she pass her love of travel to me? Did she inspire the deep and abiding friendships I have with so many women today?

Only after she died of dementia at age eighty-nine did I begin to realize that I had been granted the mother I needed. And what my mother could not impart to me was provided by many other "mothers" along the way who have lent me their guidance and love.

Throughout my life I've been given wonderful friends to share the giddy moments and help me through the most difficult times. I have three sisters, whom I admire, love and hold dear, and yet, I've turned to my girl-friends again and again for understanding when my life is at its best and worst. I rather think of them as the family of my choosing, and my other mothers.

I never really knew my mother, but looking at those old photos, I can see myself. I am like her, peering out with large, dark eyes at the world, arms linked with my friends, standing coyly on the edge of whatever comes next.

Kathy Bird

*chapter five*

# Possibility

"*The soul should always stand ajar,*
*ready to welcome the ecstatic experience*"
Emily Dickinson

# Becoming Beautiful, and Other Transformations

*"Vanity is becoming a nuisance; I can see why women give it up, eventually. But I'm not ready for that yet."*

Margaret Atwood, *Cat's Eye*

When I was in middle school, my mom converted the utility room of our brick, ranch-style house into a beauty salon. Her name is Lillian, so she called it "The Lily Pad." All during my teen years, I would come home from cheerleading practice and rummage in the fridge to a lively background soundtrack coming from behind the utility room door: the chatter and laughter that is unique to the beauty salon.

It's the sound of women becoming beautiful, or at least believing in that moment that they are; the sound of hope, encouragement, and validation—of women helping one another feel good about themselves. My mom is great at it. While she was skilled at cutting, coloring, and styling hair, she is exceptionally talented at making women feel hopeful, positive, and valued. Which is probably why, throughout my entire life, whenever I've met someone who knows her, they nearly always exclaim, "Oh, I love your mother!"

The home beauty salon was important to my mom: She wanted to be there when I came in from school, but she also wanted to earn income, define her schedule, and have something all her own. While she enjoyed

the convenience of the home business, she always dreamed of something more, her own freestanding salon, with an atmosphere that was lovely and spa-like.

When I was twenty-five, I was living in Atlanta and working as Manager of Marketing Communications for a major telecommunications company. I remember coming home from work one day and shuffling through the mail as I stood in the sunny, weedy front yard of my funky little white frame house on Lindbergh Drive in Peachtree Hills. Ripping open a letter from my mother, a photo fluttered to the grass. It was a picture of Mom, smile beaming, standing in front of her new salon. Her arm rested on a wooden signpost that read "Ashby & Company" in elegant script. On the back of the picture she had written, "Me and My Dream."

At that time, my mother was about fifty, my age now. Her youngest child was long gone from the nest, living in another city six hours away. My mom had been married at only eighteen, and became a mother just a year later. Having devoted her life to children and family, she was ready to expand her possibilities, her sense of who she was.

I remember how excited she was about opening her own salon, how energized and animated her voice became as she told me about it. She was starting a new business, taking a risk, and she couldn't quite believe she was actually doing it. At the time, while I listened politely and told her I was proud of her and said all the right things, I know I was really waiting for her to stop talking and return to the most pressing and important subject in both of our lives: me.

Like many people in their twenties, I was utterly self-centered. To be honest, I was probably worse than most. I was the center of my own sparkling universe. Having grown up the baby of the family by five years and the only daughter, I occupied that rarified echelon of the family princess. (Of course my brothers were so rowdy growing up that my parents just seemed grateful that I wasn't breaking lamps while wrestling in the family room.) I was praised and indulged a lot as a child—and I loved it! But I'll admit to being more than a bit insensitive in my teens and twenties. And at twenty-five, while independent and successful by most standards, I still had a lot of growing up to do as a human being.

But that day, reading the words "Me and My Dream" in my mother's handwriting, seeing the hopefulness in her eyes, I could feel what her salon meant to her, and how important her achievement was. I ran in the house, screen door slamming, to call my mom, excited for once not to talk about my career, my dramatic love life, my travel plans—but about Lillian Ashby, and how proud I was to be her daughter.

# Evolving

Meg is my analytical friend; whip smart with a wicked dry wit. She began her thirty year career with IBM as an intern our senior year at Rhodes, when we were suitemates in Voohries Dorm. We named our suite The Cave, and painted the shared private hallway with all manner of colorful graffiti—phrases, inside jokes, artistic doodles—whatever we were experiencing that year became part of our "mural."

Meg earned a Business degree and I majored in English, so we didn't have many classes together in our college careers. But that final autumn semester we did happen to have one, a history class in which the professor loved to jab the air with his fingers and ask rhetorical questions with a passion we found hilarious. I can't recall the context (if there was one), but one afternoon the loudly repeated question was "Just what have you evolved into?"

> *"We do not grow absolutely, chronologically. We grow sometimes in one dimension, and not in another, unevenly. We grow partially. We are relative. We are mature in one realm, childish in another. The past, present and future mingle and pull us backward, forward, or fix us in the present. We are made up of layers, cells, constellations."*
>
> Anaïs Nin, *Diary of Anaïs Nin, Vol. 4*

Returning to our suite that evening, I found that Meg had painted, in giant red letters, "Just WHAT Have You Evolved Into?" across the very top of our wall. It became our catchphrase for the year, the utility response to achievement and failing alike, usually delivered in a wry voice with a raised eyebrow. Stayed out late and skipped class? As you slunk into the bathroom to brush your teeth at noon, you might hear that question mockingly raised from Meg's room.

Meg, of course, never skipped class. She was already keeping lots of plates spinning and doing it exceedingly well. She carried a full load of classes her senior year while working twenty hours a week for IBM, doing such excellent work that she had a job offer in hand a month before graduation.

This is not to say she didn't make some missteps in her "evolution." One of my favorite memories involves Meg's discovery of a lipstick that purported to "blend with your body's chemistry once applied, magically transforming into the perfect shade to flatter your own unique skin tone!"

In the tube, it was a sickly green, but once swiped onto the lips— voila!—*your ideal, most flattering shade!* For some reason, Meg found this concept fascinating and couldn't wait to try it out.

She bounded into our suite late one Friday afternoon, IBM binders under both arms, ready for a quick change from her '80s shoulder-padded power suit into some stirrup pants and a shoulder-padded, geometric print tunic sweater for a big night out. "Where are we going?" she called, yanking the sweater over her head. As I caught sight of her face emerging from the neckline, my jaw dropped.

Her lips were a slick purplish red, not exactly flattering on my blonde, fair-skinned friend. She flashed me a garish purple grin. "Don't you love this new lipstick? So cool—it mixes with my body's pH for the perfect shade. Want to try it, Kel?"

It was one of those friendship tests that I failed. She seemed so happy with her new lipstick purchase, in such a great Friday night mood, that I couldn't bear to reveal my true opinion. And so…I let her go out that night looking like she had just eaten a grape Popsicle with no hands.

Mistakes were made, fortunately mostly in this minor category, during our evolution that year. But as I look back, they are the memories that bring the biggest smiles.

After graduation, Meg and Kathleen backpacked together through Europe, and then Meg moved to Arkansas to begin her career with IBM. I moved to Atlanta to pursue my own career, missing my friend and often wishing that she and I were working in the same city, so we could meet for dinner and I could get her advice on cutting my marketing budget, if not choosing my lipstick shade!

Today, she is Director of Mergers and Acquisitions for IBM's Software Group. She has worldwide responsibility for the successful integration of newly acquired software companies into IBM. This position followed a long career in Sales Management and Business Operations. Her various positions at IBM have taken her all over the world in pursuit of new opportunities.

Married to a fellow IBMer and the mother of two sons, Meg has an energy, an ambition and a level of accomplishment that I have always admired. She is not afraid to take on the big things, to be the leader, with all its attendant risk and responsibility. A problem solver in both life and work, she does it all with a wry, irresistible sense of humor.

The following story about her mother, Mary Waters, reveals the many facets of the woman who was my friend's first, best example of a woman's ability to fulfill all of her aspirations: personal, family and career.

According to Meg, "As we both get older, Mom continues to inspire me with how she never stops seeking, learning, and expressing herself through her poetry, writing, and spirituality. I love her sense of humor about life and all of its stages—in one of her essays she describes herself as 'being in her coffee and dessert years—rapidly approaching the after-dinner mints!' To me, whatever stage we are in, it's still sweet."

> *"It makes you wonder. All the brilliant things we might have done with our lives if only we suspected we knew how."*
>
> Ann Patchett, *Bel Canto*

# Unexpected Doors
## Meg's Story

There are some moments you don't forget. This one happened seventeen years ago in an ordinary California grocery store, as my mother and I shopped together and my three-year-old son, Alex, sat in the grocery cart. I remember how happy I was to have Mom visiting from Little Rock, and how much I was looking forward to a wonderful week of just being with her. We were talking and laughing nonstop as we loaded the cart with celebratory foods—plenty of hors d'oeuvres and white wine along with the ingredients for the special dishes that she always prepared on her visits. Alex was starting to get fussy, which meant he was receiving a ready and flowing supply of goldfish crackers to keep him occupied.

As we were nearly finished with our shopping, the dam burst. No amount of goldfish or cajoling could keep Alex quiet. He began releasing torrential screams that caused everyone in the store to stop to witness what kind of abuse this child must be suffering. When he went into a full-scale tantrum (of Richter measure), the only way out was to abandon the cart full of groceries and run for the exit.

So many times before, I had eschewed those meltdowns; all kids have them, right? But there was nothing typical about that tantrum (nor all the ones that had come before it). Nor was his lack of speech typical, or his lack of eye contact or his toe walking. I ignored so many signs due to fear of the unknown. But there he was, white-knuckling the cart and convulsing his small body, trying to overturn it and all of its contents, screaming at the top of his lungs. There was my beautiful boy with his white-blonde hair and blue eyes, who looked so much like me, so much like mom, my firstborn, the love of my life.

Deep down, I knew something was wrong, but I didn't want to know, so I kept it buried. I hoped he'd outgrow it. But now Mom was there and I was standing in the grocery store staring at a gallon of melting ice cream and three bottles of really good buttery, oaky Chardonnay, and none of that was going to matter in a few moments because Alex was about to show me and my mother something that I did not want to see.

As I clutched my screaming son in my arms and ran from the overfilled cart, I was hit with a wave of emotion. First, I was angry at Alex for his horrific and embarrassing meltdown, not only in public but in front of my mom (proving me a bad mother). But mostly, I was afraid. I suddenly saw Alex's tantrum through Mom's eyes, and I was scared to death of what might be "wrong" with my child.

When we were home and had settled Alex, Mom looked at me calmly and gave voice to the words I had kept silent. "Meg, this is not normal," she said, with stern emphasis on the NOT. "Something is wrong." As I sat huddled in my despair on the couch, Mom consulted a child development book from my bookshelf. I remember the book had a very small reference box with a list of the top ten signs of autism…of which I counted, my son had eight.

I am grateful that, in that frightening moment of recognition and acceptance, my mom was by my side. I held tightly to the lifeline of her voice, her calm, steady reassurance that Alex would be OK, that I had a son who was going to need a lot of help, but that it would get better. He would get better.

> *"One sad thing about this world is that the acts that take the most out of you are usually the ones that people never know about."*   Anne Tyler, *Celestial Navigation*

As any parent who has received an autism diagnosis knows, it is heartbreaking. You have to remind yourself to breathe, because it feels like all the oxygen has been drawn from the room. The happy future you had pictured for your child becomes a dark and confusing blur. As I sat with my acceptance, I saw doorways of possibility closing, one by one. I remember feeling profoundly sad, unlike any sadness I had ever endured.

My mom knew of this sadness, and understood it. During her career as a speech therapist, she had worked with many children with developmental disabilities. She counseled parents who had received crushing diagnoses for their beautiful children. She worked with teenagers who came from home environments fraught with abuse and neglect. She herself knew sadness, as the only child of parents who were substance abusers.

My mom was born in a small Wisconsin town on November 16, 1935,

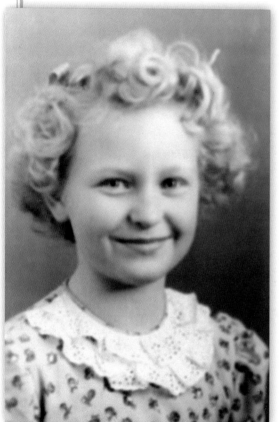

nestled between her father's birthday on November 15 and her mother's on November 17. Her dad was the town doctor, and her mother was a nurse. While her parents loved her, they struggled with raising a child. Their addictions made them haphazard parents and she learned from an early age that they were not to be relied upon. Often she would be left to wait alone for hours as her mother or father would simply forget to pick her up.

Her childhood memories are tainted with feelings of loneliness and abandonment. As a small girl, she turned to books for comfort and escape, becoming a voracious reader and writer of stories. Left alone much of the time, she liked to create stories about her sole companions, a trio of unconventional pets: Hopalong, a one-legged chicken; Peanuts, the tame squirrel; and Scampie, a deodorized skunk. She also liked to write about the colorful characters that were friends and patients of her father's. She once wrote a poem that began, "I knew the small town secrets which my father knew."

From childhood, she learned to peer below the surface of things, one reason I think that she has always possessed such extraordinary insight about people and events. Books, her earliest and truest friends, are a passion held constant all her life, and reading and creating stories are among the ways she mothered me best. I treasure the lifetime of books she has given me and poems she has written for me.

Mom grew up without many rules and the few rules she was given, she made a habit of breaking. This defiant aspect to her personality did not serve her well when her parents sent her to a Catholic boarding school in Minnesota. The nuns kept a close eye on Mom and confined her to campus on a regular basis given her penchant for noncompliance. There was one nun, Sister Timothy, who "got her" and turned out to be one of Mom's greatest influences; they remained lifelong friends until Sister Timothy's death a few years ago.

At Marquette University, Mom majored in speech pathology and met my father Bill. She remembers her college years fondly, an opportunity to spread her wings without the stifling supervision she experienced in boarding school. Her marriage was a bit of a shock to her system. She was an only child marrying a man with six siblings.

In 1957, she started her career as a speech pathologist at four local elementary schools in Virginia. One of the schools was Sojourner Truth, where she was the only white person at the school, but she never felt like an outsider, and remembers it as being her favorite. That teaching experience was the beginning of what was to be an adult life committed to working on diversity.

A move back to Milwaukee in 1959 was met with an offer to write and deliver a live television show called *Speech Time*. She knew nothing about scripting a program or appearing on TV, but she didn't let on. Despite being a young mother in the 1950s, she saw the opportunity and seized it with both hands.

She spent a fair amount of her career known as "Miss Mary", appearing on two live television shows dedicated to helping children with their speech sounds. She became pregnant twice during her show's tenure, and the TV station sat her behind a desk since it was considered "inappropriate" for a pregnant woman to appear on TV. Given her rule-breaking nature, she rallied against such nonsensical notions and found every opportunity to show off her growing pregnant belly!

Throughout my childhood, Mom immersed herself in a myriad of jobs and projects. Her boundless energy for new endeavors amazed us all. Patience was not always her strong suit, however, and as my brother Tim describes it, Mom always wants to solve problems in real time rather than due time.

Her desire to help others led her to work with disadvantaged youth, traveling the state to speak out on the subject of drug and alcohol abuse. This mission was borne from her own experience with her parents. Mom also actively worked on the subject of diversity, facilitating weekend workshops for teens and business leaders alike.

She saw potential in those who hardly knew they had it, such as a young African American student named Roosevelt Thompson, whom she profiled in an award-winning PBS documentary entitled *As We See It*. Roosevelt was a charismatic young man who had the ability to defuse racial tensions at Central High School during the turbulent seventies.

Mom saw in Roosevelt Thompson all the possibilities of a changing world. When his life was tragically cut short in an auto accident just after he received the Rhodes Scholarship in his senior year at Yale, my mother mourned his death as if she had lost one of her own children. To her and so many others, he represented the hope of an entire generation of students at Central High School.

Roosevelt's ability to get people to talk honestly about difficult subjects continued to inspire my Mom as she prepared for her "second act" when I left for college. Forever reinventing herself, she went back to school at age forty-five for her Masters in Interpersonal Communications. She used those skills to lead conversations with business, school, and civic groups on a host of topics, many of them uncomfortable. Sex, substance abuse, racial issues—nothing was ever taboo with Mom. She is not frightened to face what is difficult, what makes us anxious and afraid.

And so that day in the grocery store, she put a name to that which I was terrified to label. I'll never forget the balm of those simple, beautiful words, "It *will* be OK. *He* will be ok." Just as she perceived Roosevelt Thompson's talent decades before, my mother intuited Alex's potential.

After Alex's formal diagnosis, Mom was steadfast in her support. I am sure she sometimes felt helpless in the face of my urgent pursuit of so many treatment options, but she did not judge (at least in my presence) our uncharted plan. She was always there as a willing listener to share my burden. She talked to her physician friends, sent me articles, and shared many spiritual books to help me through. But most of all, she wrote me beautiful poems, words that usually arrived just when I needed them most. This one, called simply "Alex," was written when my son was in grade school.

*Alex, little golden boy,*
*how hard it is for us*
*to understand*
*that part of you*
*that lives in shadows.*
*But darkness can nourish*
*as well as light,*
*and as you begin to emerge,*
*you will carry the strength of the shadow,*
*and it will serve you well.*
*We have lessons to learn*
*from you;*
*far greater, I think,*
*than those you will learn*
*from us.*

Her unbridled support and encouraging words carried us through some dark moments as my husband and I worked to assemble the best set of services possible to help our son. Some treatments have been more successful than others, but none of them a cure. Because there is no cure for autism. But my mother was right. Alex is OK. His life hasn't been easy, but just as she predicted, things *did* get better.

His life may be different from what I had once imagined for him, but Alex is growing, learning, and working to fulfill his potential. As a senior in high school, he was asked to record a video to help students at his high school understand the consequences of bullying and his autism. In the video, my son, who once could barely make eye contact, is standing tall and looking steadily into the camera, saying, "I was bullied. I felt left out. They ignored me and made me feel bad. But then my mom came in and talked to the class about my disability and things got better."

When I saw that footage for the first time, I thought my heart would burst with love and joy. Of course, no one was more proud than Mom. Alex is indeed her grandchild, bravely standing up, sharing his story, and speaking for those who could not do so for themselves. That's quite a legacy.

Mom has cheered Alex's hard-won progress through the years as he has become more and more independent. She recently wrote him a beautiful letter of support on his twentieth birthday. In it, she wrote, "Your path has not been an easy one we know, but you have walked it with grace, love, and kindness. Alex, you have become a fine young man, and we will continue to enjoy watching your life unfold, as you aim for the stars, one by one, day by day, and reach them."

When our son John was born, Mom built a special relationship with him as well. Through their playful exchange of loving insults, I see my own relationship with my mom being reinvented. John is a good writer like his Grandma. I hope all the "left brains" in our family don't squash this special talent of his. He also has a deep compassionate streak that was likely inherited from her as well.

Mom encourages my sons in their every endeavor, just as she encouraged me at their age. Whether it was acting in school plays, writing and editing for the school newspaper, cheerleading, attending cotillion, practicing gymnastics, holding class office or leading church retreats, she was a staunch supporter. I think she knew that I liked to keep a lot of plates spinning, much as she had. Mom always let me make my own decisions, but I would blame her for the bad ones anyway!

Her words of support are reflected in her poem to me titled "Megrit" written soon after Alex's diagnosis.

*When you feel sad,*
*powerless,*
*overwhelmed,*
*and yet are able*
*to rise above*
*or circumvent*
*those feelings,*
*and act to change*
*the situation,*
*the soul takes note.*
*And, in time,*
*help will come,*
*and strength, and peace.*
*One day,*
*You will realize*
*that you have been*
*forever changed,*
*and that you have grown up,*
*not merely grown old.*

Since her retirement, my tireless mother has written five books of poetry and essays, the creative expression of over thirty-five years of exploring her spirituality and seeking to understand life's greater purpose. In the first, *Sandpaper Blankets*, she inscribed, "To Meg – my daughter and friend – the first person to call me 'poet.'" I liked that.

Having a freethinking, truth-speaking poet for a mother is not always easy, but whenever there is news, good or bad, the first phone call I make is to her. I know on the other end of the line will be a loving, encouraging voice poised to listen like no other, the voice of my mother. My sister Kathie describes those phone calls as "talking each other to a better place, where we all take turns on the ledge." When it is my turn, I am grateful that she is holding the line.

Helen Baeza

# chapter six

# Motherhood

"To her whose heart is my heart's quiet home,
To my first Love, my Mother, on whose knee
I learnt love-lore that is not troublesome;
Whose service is my special dignity,
And she my loadstar while I go and come. . ."
Christina Rossetti

# A Little Motherly Advice

Margaret and I became friends in the halls of Williford Dorm the very first week of our freshman year. She fell in love with a boy named Lee that same autumn, and married him the summer after our college graduation. They have four children, three sons and one daughter, the youngest.

With four, Margaret has the most children of our group and she became a mother the earliest, at twenty-five. I was second to become a mom, at twenty-nine. The rest of our group wouldn't have children until their thirties and early forties, so Margaret has always been our go-to girl for advice on all things motherhood.

I was tempted to follow Margaret's lead into what I consider "big family" territory, in hopes of having a girl for baby number four, just as she had. My own mother encouraged me to go for it. We have always had a wonderful, close relationship and I know she wanted me to experience that singular bond with a daughter of my own.

When I was younger, the thought of not being able to mother a little girl, to share the treasures I had loved and saved from my own childhood—the Barbies, ballet costumes, and Little House on the Prairie books—sometimes made me feel a bit wistful. To those reading this who think I should have tried to raise my sons in a more progressive, gender-neutral fashion, believe me, I tried. I have the headless Barbies to prove it! (And the only chapter my boys ever let me read aloud from *Little House in the Big Woods* was the one about Pa shooting the bear.)

I was certainly not unfamiliar with the particular rites and passages of boys. I grew up with two older brothers, five and six years my senior, both of whom I adore and am very close with today. We still celebrate nearly all the big holidays together, and our children share a loving bond. My sons don't even consider it a true holiday unless they can get together with their "cousins by the dozens" in both the Ashby and Paul clans…and the Fourth of July is simply a bore if Uncle Jeff and Uncle David don't create some kind of memorable mayhem with their fireworks extravaganzas at the lake.

Growing up, the term "rowdy" didn't begin to describe my brothers. They were always "rough-housing," as my mom called it—yelling, wrestling, and throwing balls through windows. There were lots of concussions, casts, stitches, and teeth being knocked out in everything from sledding accidents (David) to being caught on a barbed wire fence (Jeff). My mom made no secret of the fact that she was over-the-moon grateful for me, her girl, and we were our own little team throughout my childhood.

I remember a woman with four rambunctious sons whom my brothers were friends with when we were growing up, when all the neighborhood kids spent endless summer days outside, playing sandlot baseball or riding bikes. "Poor Mrs. M.," my mom would sigh, shaking her head, "all those

> *"Before becoming a mother I had a hundred theories on how to bring up children. Now I have seven children and only one theory: love them, especially when they least deserve to be loved."* Kate Samperi

boys and no daughter…" I grew up thinking that being a "poor Mrs. M." was a fate worse than death, bringing you nothing but pity, piles of smelly laundry and bills for broken windows.

My mom grew up poor, with no money for extras like music or ballet lessons, so she enthusiastically signed me up for everything. She was my biggest fan at dance recitals and school musicals, always sending flowers backstage and bragging to people about my exceptional talent and grace. ("She was surely wearing her 'mom goggles,'" I can just hear my son Robert saying dryly as I write this. And he would be utterly correct.)

Mom and I both love fashion and home décor, and are enjoying our fifth decade of joint shopping expeditions, just yesterday to TJ Maxx, where my mom, as usual, waved an outfit in front of me that "looks just like you!" Growing up, she would often tiptoe into my room early and whisper conspiratorially, "Let's just call you in sick to school today and we'll go shopping and out to lunch in Bowling Green—just the two of us!"

Now she denies this of course, saying it only happened once, or maybe twice, and that I exaggerate everything just like Grandma Julia. But how often we played hooky together doesn't matter; what matters is the sweetness of those long days, those memories.

Like no one else in the world, my mom makes me feel truly seen and understood. In her presence, I feel loved. Isn't that what most of us want? To be seen and grasped with so much love that we are interpreted only as our finest, worthiest selves?

Having been so close to my mother and my grandmother, I thought I needed a daughter in order to feel that same level of maternal connection and intimacy, but I was wrong. Like so many things in life, the gifts I received from motherhood were unexpected, and richer than anything I could have imagined or chosen for myself.

I thought I would miss getting to recreate my favorite girlhood memories, but instead I was given new experiences and traditions to savor. I thought I might miss creating dollhouses with a daughter, but I didn't know how much more fun it could be to build forts. Barbies pale in comparison to superheroes. After all, you can transform yourself into a caped crusader with a well-placed towel and a safety pin.

The treehouse Rand and the boys built for their "Maniac Monkey" adventures has rotted and fallen down now, but the memories of three little boys whooping through the backyard, playing pirates and battling Darth Vader with light sabers, is still golden in my memory.

(But don't get me started on Star Wars. Somehow I missed the phenomenon in the seventies and eighties, but not the second time around! My sons helped me tap into my inner sci-fi fan, and today my arcane knowledge of Star Wars trivia would impress George Lucas himself.)

My boys have brought me so much laughter and joy. Whether jumping off sand dunes, creating a slippery slide down the back hill or building elaborate Lego and Hot Wheels superhighways, their energy and enthusiasm always made the days sparkle with life, and I loved being part of their adventures as a young mom.

Their baseball card collections and sports trophies are starting to collect dust, but perhaps they will be handed down one day, just as Rand and my brother Jeff have passed on their own special cards to our boys. (But I'm saving the doll Grandma brought me back from Ireland too, just in case.)

Antonio Cesar

I only get to listen to our sons playing guitar together in the basement on holidays now, and like every other mother in history, I savor the music, feeling melancholy surprise at how fleeting and ephemeral their childhood was.

Over the years, I have shared many of the joys and worries of raising boys with my friend Margaret. I have always been grateful for the fact that her three sons are older than my own, so I can get free counsel on every mystifying detail about mothering boys from a smart woman who has been in the trenches.

As our children enter young adulthood, our conversations about them now are more about college majors, girlfriends, and job prospects than lost baby teeth, the playground bully or best Halloween costumes, but I still seek and value her opinions. The best advice she ever gave me? "Don't overreact." My sons would probably say I failed on that one, but I sure tried.

Margaret is smart and straightforward, and while we sometimes

JoAnn Abdelwahabe

disagree, I usually find myself following her advice. She is both an inspired cook and excellent photographer, two talents that our group of friends enjoys on our reunion trips. I'm still making some of the recipes she sent me after our Colorado reunion more than fifteen years ago, my family's favorites being her Baked Chicken and Orzo and Grilled Peanut Chicken.

Margaret's cooking, writing and artistic abilities all come together beautifully on her blog, "The Right Recipe," in which she shares the creative joy of cooking for family and friends. Her love of good food and creating meaningful traditions around the table is rooted in her memories of big family dinners at the home of her southern grandmother, whom everyone called "Mur."

I had met her grandmother once, on a drive through Mississippi, but it was only after reading Margaret's lovely tribute that I truly understood the many similarities between this strong and graceful Southern matriarch and my own dear friend.

# The Grace And Conviction
# of a Mississippi Matriarch
## Margaret's Story

To celebrate the first birthday of each child, grandchild, and great-grandchild, my grandmother would have his or her portrait framed in gold and hung along her staircase hallway. At the time of her death in 2002, at age ninety-three, there were portraits of her four children, nineteen grandchildren, and forty-five great-grandchildren hanging on her walls. In the closet, she had stored five extra frames for the future but she would have needed many more. She now has sixty-six great-grandchildren.

The term matriarch comes to mind but she was so much more than that. A true steel magnolia, a strong and resilient woman who, if born in another place and time, would surely have been a force to reckon with in business, politics, philanthropy, education, or whatever she put her mind to. She was a woman from a small town in Mississippi who lived a life

of grace and conviction, and she had a profound influence on her family, friends and community.

I am number four of the nineteen grandchildren of Catherine Cameron Wilkerson Bryan, known as "Kitty" to her friends and to her family as "Mur" (pronounced "Muh"). She had a beautiful southern drawl, the kind that turns "sister" into "sista" and "Margaret" into "Maugret."

I was her favorite grandchild. Or so I thought. I have come to learn that most of us felt that we were her favorite. That was one of her gifts, I suppose. She made you feel special.

Mur was born in the Delta—Greenville, Mississippi, to be exact. She was the oldest of five and spent her early childhood living at Clifton Plantation, a cotton plantation farmed by sixty black families. This makes her a member of the last generation to experience that particular cultural upbringing. Her education began in a one-room schoolhouse in Winterville then continued in Greenville until her graduation in 1927.

She spoke of the year 1927 often, in great detail, as that was the year of The Flood, when the levee broke at Mound Landing just eight miles north of her house and the Mississippi River inundated Greenville. She told us stories about the water rising in the streets, how she had to hold onto tables and was rescued from the rooftop of a building and taken to Vicksburg by riverboat.

Her stories were dramatic but I'm afraid that I didn't truly appreciate the scope of the disaster until years later when I read *Rising Tide, the Great Mississippi Flood of 1927 and How it Changed America* by John M. Barry. Mur and her family evacuated to Memphis, Tennessee, and took refuge on the campus of Southwestern at Memphis, now Rhodes College, for four months. (Perhaps this is one reason why, twenty-seven years later, she would insist that my father attend Southwestern at Memphis when he really just wanted to go to Ole Miss with his friends.)

After a postponed graduation due to the flood, she enrolled in Mississippi State College for Women, also known as "The W," where she majored in Spanish and Latin. At her funeral, my father told of the time that Mur and a few of her friends at "The W" were outraged to learn that Theodore

"If nothing is going well,
call your grandmother."

Italian Proverb

Bilbo, the notoriously racist governor of Mississippi, was handing out the diplomas at their graduation. In protest, they refused to step up onto the stage to receive their diplomas from him, a very bold move at that time.

After college, Mur became a social worker and earned an advanced degree from Tulane University. She met my grandfather when she, on behalf of a needy family, was trading in some government issued oxen for a pair of mules, which were apparently more useful animals. My grandfather conducted the transaction and they married 100 days later at the courthouse after work.

I asked her once if she felt like she knew him well enough at that point and she said, "Oh, yes. We had dated twice a week for three months." She was twenty-six years old and, according to Mur, her parents were surprised, as they thought she would never marry.

Mur was extremely active in her community, the small town of West Point, Mississippi. When she learned that people were traveling for miles to find school programs for their disabled children, she built The Catherine Bryan School for Special Children on the property next to her own home.

Mur was elected Mississippi Mother of the Year in 1970 and in a short autobiography she wrote for the occasion, she said, "My husband, my children and I worked hard to help ease the integration of the public schools. We believe in public school education and all of our grandchildren attend public school today."

In 1980, when her beloved First Presbyterian Church voted to secede from the national Presbyterian Church (USA), because of some of the national church's liberal social views (women ministers, for example), Mur was eighty years old. She could have joined the local Methodist Church, where many in her family were members. Instead she, along with twenty other parishioners, purchased a small house on Main Street, hired a female minister, invited black members, and founded their own place of worship. The church remains today, still small and still affiliated with the national Presbyterian Church.

My father, reflecting upon his mother and her ideals, calls her "an unreconstructed Democrat," and adds, "Mother's attachment to the Democrats came about, in part, because of her early career as a social worker during the Great Depression. It also emanated from her strong identity with the politics of her nineteenth-century agrarian forebearers. Neither of these points, however, really explains her liberal social views. I suppose they were simply an inherent trait."

As I turn fifty and watch my children grow and move away, I find myself thinking about Mur's role in our family, and how she was able to draw us together in such an important and meaningful way. Mur was big on traditions and we, as a family, had a lot of them. There were those first year portraits, of course, but there were many more.

We ate Sunday dinner at her house every week. We lined up oldest to youngest to go through the buffet line, which always included "Mur's Rice," a ham or turkey, various casseroles, maybe a Jell-O salad and either cornbread muffins or those soft, pull-apart rolls that come in a heat-and-eat package.

On Valentine's Day, she sent each of us a Valentine in the mail, just a small one, like the ones you buy in a box to give to your classmates in elementary school, and it was always signed, "Guess Who?" And each year, tucked inside your birthday card from Mur was a $15 or $25 check, depending on your age. When we married, our spouses also started receiving a birthday check.

Mur and my grandfather took their grandchildren, two by two, on a special trip. It was nothing fancy, maybe a trip to Hot Springs, Arkansas or to see Mammoth Cave in Kentucky. She also assigned each of her grandchildren something to collect. I collected paperweights, my cousins had spoons, music boxes, etc. Perhaps this was her way of having something special to do and talk about with each of us…or maybe it was just to make Christmas shopping for nineteen grandchildren easier!

Christmas, of course, had its own ritual celebrations and traditions. There was her annual "Cookie Party" a week before Christmas. She made slice-and-bake sugar cookies and topped some of them with red and green sprinkles and some with a single pecan half. I thought they were amazing— proving that you don't have to be Martha Stewart to create special holiday memories. And on Christmas Eve, we all spent the night at her house so we could wake up together and see what Santa left, even though we all lived within a few minutes of one another.

She wasn't an outwardly emotional person. My father says he never saw her cry. She commanded respect in a quiet way. I remember when I was staying with her in the summer of 1984 and I left several times to go visit my boyfriend, who lived a few hours' drive away. I had a car and he didn't.

One day at breakfast, Mur looked at me matter-of-factly and with absolutely no hint of disapproval said, "In my day, it was the boy's responsibility to come visit the girl." Of course, I was on the phone right away telling the boy to borrow a car and get down there because I couldn't bear the thought that Mur might think poorly of us!

When my firstborn came along and Mur saw how frustrated I was that he cried constantly, she told me, "I wouldn't give a nickel for a baby that didn't fuss." And oddly enough, that was the one thing said to me during that time that made me feel a little bit easier about the situation.

Mur died of old age. She had outlived all her younger siblings. She said to me once that all of her friends were dead. She didn't say it in a depressed way, just as a fact, and it was true. The last time I saw her, it was obvious that her little body (she was just 5'2") was tired, her skin almost translucent.

And although she couldn't really speak well at that point, I could tell that she recognized me by the way she stared into my eyes. And I knew that if she had the strength, she could still explain who my second cousins twice removed are, and describe the color of the dress she wore to that fancy dinner in New York City thirty years earlier. I wasn't overcome with sadness when she died two weeks later. You can't argue with ninety-three.

I've often wondered if Mur's sons- and daughters-in-law might have resented some of the obligations that come with being part of the tightly knit Bryan family. It would be understandable. But what I do know is that, as a child, there was great comfort in those traditions and routines. And even though I don't see all my cousins and aunts and uncles as much as I would like now, I have never once lost the feeling that I have an awful lot of people in this world who love me and will always be there for me no matter what. And I believe much of that feeling comes from the environment that she created for us as children.

I once interviewed Mur for a college psychology project and I asked her to tell me what she liked most about herself. She struggled with this question, paused for quite a while and then said, "I like that I don't interfere with my children's lives." She elaborated by saying that she would give her opinion if asked, but that she was never judgmental, even if she felt that a mistake was being made.

As a mother of four myself, I certainly know how hard that can be, but I am just now beginning to realize how important it is. So maybe that is one of the crucial ingredients in the recipe for a loving family. Led by the example set by my grandmother, I aspire to figure out the rest.

> *"There were two things about Mama.*
> *One is she always expected the best out of me.*
> *And the other is that then no matter what I did,*
> *whatever I came home with, she acted like it was the moon*
> *I had just hung up in the sky and plugged in all the stars.*
> *Like I was that good."*
>
> Barbara Kingsolver, *The Bean Trees*

Gennie Darisme

# chapter seven

# Wisdom

"*I long to put the experience of fifty years at once into your young lives, to give you at once the key of that treasure chamber every gem of which has cost me tears and struggles and prayers, but you must work for these inward treasures yourselves.*"

Harriet Beecher Stowe
to her twin daughters, 1861

# Illuminating Facets

*"I remembered that the real world was wide, and that a varied field of hopes and fears, of sensations and excitements, awaited those who had the courage to go forth into its expanse, to seek real knowledge of life amidst its perils."*

Charlotte Brontë, *Jane Eyre*

Last year when I was going through a challenging time, my nephew Kyle Ashby, a pilot in the US Navy, sent me a wonderful book called *The Prodigal God*, by Tim Keller. In his book, Keller quotes C.S. Lewis from an essay he wrote called, "Friendship."

Keller writes, "[C.S.] Lewis was part of a famous circle of friends called The Inklings, which included JRR Tolkien, and also the author Charles Williams, whose sudden death inspired this quote:

> *"In each of my friends there is something that only some other friend can fully bring out. By myself I am not large enough to call the whole man into activity. I want other lights than my own to show all his facets. Now that Charles is dead, I shall never again see Ronald's [Tolkien's] reaction to a specifically Charles joke. Far from having more of Ronald, having him 'to myself' now that Charles is away, I have less of Ronald... In this, Friendship exhibits a glorious 'nearness by resemblance' to heaven itself where the very multitude of the blessed... increases the fruition which each of us has of God."*

To me, this beautiful quote sums up how it feels to be part of a tapestry of friends, with a multi-layered weave of history connecting us. It takes "other lights than my own" to reveal all their sparkling facets, and I don't find it surprising that Lewis missed the sound of his friends' shared laughter most of all.

I love Anne Lamott's description of laughter as "carbonated holiness," and, like most people, I absolutely love to laugh. When I return from a reunion with my friends, my abs feel as if they've been through a fitness boot camp from all the laughing. As with any close group, something typically happens that becomes the theme of the gathering and a touchstone for laughter for years to come. One year, it involved the premature use of the now quite welcomed word, "Ma'am"…

We were in our mid-thirties, and my friend Meg organized an active long weekend near her home in Northern California, complete with hiking, wine tasting, and a rafting trip down the Truckee River. As we dutifully filled out our waivers absolving the rafting company of responsibility should we lose our lives among the rapids, we couldn't help but notice (being only human) how cute the young guys renting out the rafts were. Unfortunately, as they were handing us our oars and life jackets, one of them said in a polite voice, "Here you go, Ma'am." We were, of course, horrified. Surely we weren't old enough to be addressed in this humiliating fashion? Did we look like their mothers already?

Egos deflated, we bravely battled the rushing rapids and jagged rocks in our little yellow raft that afternoon. Each time we avoided a near-death experience someone would yell out, "They called us Ma'am!" and we'd all burst into astonished, indignant laughter. I suppose the moral of that story is: if you're gonna get old, it's best to do it with friends who can help you find the humor in life's inevitable blows to your vanity.

Of our group, Meg and Kathleen are the funniest ones. They were roommates for three years, and no one can make Meg laugh like Kathleen. I understand what Lewis meant about "having less of Ronald without Charles," for I wouldn't have the same experience of Meg without Kathleen there to bring it out. On our trips, they usually room together. As I fall asleep listening to their banter about who corrupted whom in

college, I'm almost transported to their first dorm room at Bellingrath Hall.

Raised in Florence, Alabama, Kathleen has a broad Southern accent and a beautiful, even broader smile that warms you up inside. Sporty and athletic, she has a big laugh and loves to punctuate her stories with lots of Deep South expressions like LAWDY! And GIRL! And PALEEZE! Just the sight of one of her text messages makes me laugh, as half the words are all caps, heavy on the emoticons, with at least one LAWDY. As I write this, I can hear her voice in my head, and I cannot help smiling.

Kathleen has devoted thirty years to a career in education, teaching high school English and coaching volleyball and tennis, bringing her sense of humor, compassion, and love for young people into her classroom every day. A lifelong learner, she received her Master's Degree in Education from the University of Alabama in 1990.

I chose Wisdom as the theme for Kathleen's chapter, not just because she is an educator, but because of the story of her two biggest childhood influences: her grandmother Martha and her family's longtime housekeeper, Ruby.

As we collaborated on her essay, Kathleen sent me audio files of interviews she did with Ruby shortly after they celebrated Ruby's ninetieth birthday together. I was struck by their similar sense of humor, the shared memories that got them both laughing at precisely the same moment, and the beautiful Southern cadences of their mingled voices. In their teasing banter, I could hear the beginnings of my friend's love of laughter.

As I listened to the recordings, I could also sense the forged memories between them, the lessons taught and learned, and the deep respect that Kathleen has for Ruby, a woman who gave her so much love, guidance, and wisdom, despite living in a society that did not value her contributions at the time.

Kathleen later told me that when she walked into her house after Ruby's party that day, her phone was already ringing. It was Ruby, wanting to make sure that "her baby" had arrived home safely. "At ninety, she is still worrying about me, along with so many others. She is still giving. I don't know of anyone with a greater capacity for love than Ruby Wilson."

# Lessons
## Kathleen's Story

*"There are some things you learn best in calm, and some in storm."*
Willa Cather, *The Story of the Lark*

I am a teacher. From early childhood, it's what I have always known that I wanted to do. My passion is teaching and coaching teenagers. I love seeing "the light" come on when my students understand a new concept, and after twenty-eight years, I still consider it a privilege and a blessing to go to school every day!

It is both an exciting responsibility and an honor to have the opportunity to make a difference in a young life. And when I think of the people who have shaped and guided my own, I think of two exceptionally wise women who taught me early lessons in compassion, determination, resilience, and perhaps most important, forgiveness.

Martha Louise Little Albritton and Ruby Wilson Hodges loved me, set examples of strong womanhood for me, and corrected me when I needed it. Their powerful influence lives today in all aspects of my life, professionally, personally, and spiritually.

## Baba

My grandmother, Martha Louise Little Albritton, was born in 1903 in Sparta, Tennessee. Like me, she was both an educator and a college athlete. She began her career teaching English at Board Valley School, a one-room schoolhouse with approximately twenty students. From an early age, I saw similarities in us and always wanted to make her proud.

As a young woman in the 1920s, she played college basketball for Tennessee Tech. I love the picture of her in the team uniform—a sailor-style middy blouse and bloomers—holding a basketball. There is a defiant sparkle in her eye as she confidently holds the ball in front of her with out-stretched arms. She always encouraged me as an athlete and was so excited when I went on to play volleyball and tennis for Rhodes College.

In our family, Martha Albritton was always larger than life. Even as a small child I remember being impressed by her multiple careers in teaching and business, her world travels, and her accomplishments in sports and philanthropy. As I spent time with her during long summer days at her lake house, I realized that those goals and ambitions were inside of me, too.

She was an early female pioneer in the radio industry as both a successful manager and owner, and her work took her all over the world. She fell in love with China and fascinated us with her stories and pictures from "the Orient." For small-town kids in Florence, Alabama, in the late '60s and '70s, my grandmother exuded a glamour and worldliness like no one else.

We grandkids called her Baba, and I think even as children we somehow recognized that she was a woman before her time, a trailblazer who pursued new outlets for her creativity and ambition right up until her death at eighty-six. As a young girl I loved riding in her golf cart, listening to her stories about sports and travel. Baba took up golf at age sixty and regularly won tournaments up until her eighties, beating women decades her junior. On August 23, 1967, one day past her sixty-fourth birthday, she even made a hole in one! Her golf carts were always red, like her fingernail and toenail polish, the front doors on her homes, and most of her clothes. Her favorite color reflected her energetic personality, sporty enthusiasm, and cheeky self-confidence.

When my grandmother was in her early 40s, she and my grandfather Sam built the first radio station in McMinnville, Tennessee. He was busy with his successful dental prac-tice, so the radio business was her responsibility and she poured all of her considerable energy into it.

It was 1947, and it was unusual for a woman to be known for her hard-nosed business sense. When the local drugstore owner didn't pay his advertising bills, she marched into his store and helped herself to items off the shelves until she thought it totaled the amount she was owed! Under her management, the station was a huge success and they went on to build another station in Sparta, naming it WSMT—the "S" for Sam and "M" for Martha. In the 1950s she became one of the founding members of American Women in Radio and Television.

When her youngest sister died of polio in 1949, a devastated Martha was determined to transform her grief into a cure for polio. She was state fundraising chairperson and later became national fundraising chairperson for Infantile Paralysis and the March of Dimes, working extensively with actress Helen Hayes and foundation president Basil O'Connor to raise money for research. When Baba believed in something, she took action.

To have accomplished all that she did in a time when so few women were in business or leadership positions at all, let alone owners and manag-ers, is a great source of pride and inspiration. To me, she was the embod-iment of how to be competitive and ambitious, but without hard edges. I can feel her spirit and drive within me, and as I enter the next phase in life, I'm pursuing new avenues to employ my "Baba genes" in ways that can hopefully improve the lives of others. I strive to be like Baba, who found a way to connect her heart to everything that she did.

# Ruby

*"I think there's just one kind of folks. Folks"*

Harper Lee, *To Kill a Mockingbird*

The other woman who shaped and influenced me is, thankfully, still in my life today. As I drove to her ninetieth birthday party last month, it occurred to me that, now that my parents have passed, Ruby Wilson Hodges has been part of my life longer than anyone else. I am grateful for that, as she continues to teach and inspire me.

Ruby was born on April 26, 1924, into a much harsher world than the one my grandmother knew. As one of ten children born to poor African American farmers in Cloverdale, Alabama, Ruby had to quit school in the eighth grade because the walk was over twelve miles each way, and her parents needed her help on the farm.

Ruby came to work for my parents in the summer of 1964 when my younger brother Will was born, and I was just a year old. Her kind and nurturing presence was a constant during my childhood, and I can still see her sitting on the end of my twin bed, a sturdy brush in hand, saying, "Tilt back yo head, honey," while she brushed my long, thick brown hair into two tight pigtails, tying on some red yarn for a touch of femininity.

Ruby was my Calpurnia, and I was her Scout, an active tomboy stair-stepped between two brothers. She was determined to insulate me from the racism in our small southern town during the 1960s and 1970s. Because of Ruby's lessons in respect and compassion, I never saw color. During this time, segregated schools still existed, hired maids entered homes from side or back doors, and the black community lived on the west side of town off Cherokee Street in small, white project homes.

Most mornings, attempting to teach me to be more ladylike, Ruby would try to convince me to wear a dress, and I would counter with the fact that it would just get dirty as I played on the swing set with my brothers, hiked the drainage alley in our back yard, or climbed trees with the neighborhood boys. She would hold out a simple play dress that all the nice little girls

wore—and I would reject it as senseless, nonfunctional, and a waste. Most photographs of my later years prove that Ruby eventually gave up that battle: I'm usually sporting cutoff denim shorts, T-shirts, and striped tube socks up to my knees!

Ruby knew that I would eventually outgrow my tomboy ways, and that how I dressed wasn't nearly as important as shaping my character and teaching me the importance of treating all people with respect. But she teases me now that she did despair that I would never learn to behave like a "young lady," no matter how hard she tried. And she did try!

One of her early lessons in ladylike behavior, not to mention impulse control, came when I was about nine. I had been crawdad hunting in the creek with my best friend, Paul. We put our catch in his mother's birdbath for safekeeping while we went back to hunt for more. While we were gone, Paul's older brother Bo tipped over the birdbath and killed all of our crawdads. When we returned later to discover the deed, Bo started to bully and badger Paul.

> *"I split my knuckle to the bone on his front teeth. My left impaired, I sailed in with my right."*
>
> Harper Lee, *To Kill a Mockingbird*

Like Scout, I pounced on Bo and gave him a bloody nose, something that made me enormously proud. Paul enjoyed seeing his brother get bloodied by a girl, but Ruby most definitely did not! When she heard the news, she marched me over and made me apologize, lecturing me the whole way down the sidewalk about how young ladies are supposed to behave.

While my own experience growing up in the Deep South of the '60s and '70s is filled with memories of endless warm days spent outside barefooted, and humid evenings scampering after lightning bugs, it was a different and much harsher world for my beloved Ruby. I might have remained ignorant of that difference until I was much older if not for her lessons in understanding, fairness, and the inherent dignity of all people. She helped me see the world through more than my own limited, comfortable experience.

While my parents were raising their four children in a non-racist home, the state of Alabama was one of the last to enforce equal rights for African Americans, and in our small town a few miles north of Birmingham, things were slow to change. In the autumn of 1973, I was in the fourth grade at JW Powell Elementary, a public school nestled in a quiet neighborhood. I remember clearly the day young black children were bused to our school, lined up in the halls, divided into groups, and marched into classrooms. At nine, I was aware enough to know that the production made on that day signified something very important in our nation's history.

After school that day, like most days, I ate my snack and talked to Ruby as she ironed clothes. It was what I unconsciously thought of as "Ruby time," just the two of us. She was a good listener, and from the time I was old enough to talk, she was the one with whom I shared my secrets.

That afternoon, I remember telling her, "Some colored kids were brought over to our school and now I have some in my class. They look

different. And they act different, too." She got quiet for a second, and put down the iron. She looked at me and said in her usual kind voice, but a voice of correction, "Honey, we is not colored…we is black. And just cause peoples have different skin color don't mean they's different on the inside. Peoples is people. It don't matter if they's black, white, red, yellow, or purple, all peoples should be treated with kindness cause they's all God's chirren." I felt embarrassed, and suddenly afraid that I had offended her. Until that moment, it hadn't occurred to me that these could be Ruby's own kids. I nodded and said, "Yes Ma'am. I will remember that."

In the spring of my sixth grade year, I forgot what Ruby had taught me, that "peoples is people." My fiercely competitive side got the best of me at our annual end of the year JW Powell School Field Day. Since the third grade, I had proudly claimed the title of "fastest girl in my grade," placing first in the fifty-yard dash, seventy-five yard dash, and six-hundred yard run-walk every year. My proud father would even close his dental practice for the afternoon on Field Day, just to come watch me run. I always looked forward to seeing his smiling face, cheering me on, and I can still hear him yelling, "Run, Kathleen, Run!"

But on that particular field day, my title came crashing down. Simply put, I got smoked in every running event by a quiet little black girl named

Mildred Oakley. Mildred had transferred to JW Powell that year, and she was in my class—a cute, petite girl who was very shy and always played by herself. Walking in the front door that day, angry and dejected, I flopped on the couch to sulk, hoping for some tender consolation and comfort from Ruby. "What's the matter which you, honey?" she asked me. "I'm mad cause I got beat in every running event at field day by this colored girl named Mildred," I told her, adding spitefully, "I don't like her."

Ruby walked over and sat next to me on the couch. She didn't put her arm around me or love on me like I wanted her to. Instead, she quietly but firmly reminded me about not using the word "colored," and then started asking me questions about Mildred. "First, you gots beat fair and square," she said matter-of-factly. "Don't do no good to be mad. And second, Mildred sounds like a very nice girl, and I bet she needs some friends. Did you ever think how scared she might be leaving her old school and coming to strange new one? Maybe that why she's so quiet-like. Kathleen, I wants you to put yoself in her shoes and think how you would feel if you had to go to a new school with mostly all black chirren." In that moment, I saw myself in Ruby's eyes, and I was ashamed.

The next day, with Ruby's soft voice in my head, I asked Mildred if she wanted to play at recess, and from that day forward, we became friends. She was an incredible athlete and we played sports together for our school teams all throughout middle and high school.

In so many ways, Ruby was my first teacher. In the slow, unhurried days of my childhood, she gave me time, wisdom, and love. She taught me to look beyond my own comfortable life and needs, to be compassionate. She taught me that, in the words of Harper Lee, *"You never really understand a person until you consider things from his point of view…Until you climb inside of his skin and walk around in it."*

As an educator, Ruby's lessons have made me a stronger, more effective teacher as I work with children from all walks of life. As a friend, they have made me a better and more compassionate listener. As a mother, her voice reminds me to teach my sons never to be quick to judge or discount, to see beyond the surface, and that a little humility is good for us all.

Malorie Cirillo

"*Accepting oneself does not preclude an attempt to become better.*"
Flannery O'Connor
*The Habit of Being: Letters of Flannery O'Connor*

Emily Strange

*chapter eight*

# Loss

"*Sorrow fully accepted brings its own gifts. For there is alchemy in sorrow. It can be transmuted into wisdom, which, if it does not bring joy, can yet bring happiness.*"

Pearl S. Buck
*The Child Who Never Grew*

# Arrivals and Departures

I felt a mix of exhilaration and terror back in August of 1981, as my dad parked our enormous olive-green Olds Ninety-Eight in front of Williford Dorm. I was arriving at Rhodes College, a five-hour drive away from home, where I knew not a soul. As my parents and I unloaded boxes and began trekking up the stairs, I could hear shrieks of happy recognition as returning girls were reunited. Like me, the new freshmen were looking shyly around, their parents awkwardly nodding to each other.

My own parents wore big smiles but their eyes seemed too bright somehow, with the unnatural patina of tears restrained by sheer will. I couldn't wait for them to leave. They lingered. Mom patted the pillows on the bed she had insisted on making up; dad chatted with other fathers and helped cart their boxes. I knew if my parents commenced with a big meaningful goodbye I was going to lose it, would start crying and wouldn't stop, and we'd all end up checking into the Memphis Holiday Inn together.

And then my new roommate walked in the door. Her name was Blair Gatewood, and she was from Atlanta, which sounded glamorous and exciting to a small town girl like me. She was tall, with curly reddish-brown hair, big green eyes, and freckles. She had a sincere smile and seemed shy, but so did I for a change—both of us feeling awkward in front of our two looming sets of parents who were peppering the atmosphere of the tiny dorm room with their friendly getting-to-know-you questions.

Blair's mother was poised, elegant, and a little intimidating. Her voice carried the intonations of her native Georgia, pronouncing her daughter's name with two syllables and a soft "h" at the end. That afternoon would be the only time I'd ever see Blair's father, but I'll never forget his warmth and wide smile, and the way he bear-hugged his daughter, my new roommate.

Just when I thought we had exhausted all possible unpacking, tidying, and cheerful advice giving, my own father suddenly wanted to take a walk with me, "just the two of us." No! I thought. This cannot get any worse. My parents weren't big on life lesson talks. My mom never even told me about "becoming a woman," for goodness sakes! (Even worse, she seemed vaguely embarrassed when I finally brought it up—at thirteen.) So what in the world did my dad want to talk to me about *alone*? Please God, don't let it be about boys, I remember praying silently.

Despite his hearty college dad demeanor, I noticed a kind of sagging quality to his broad shoulders that set off alarm bells in my brain. I quickly revised my prayers into an alternating mantra of "Please don't let my parents be getting a divorce" and "Please don't let my parents have cancer." We walked through the park-like campus in the Memphis heat, my palms sweating, and sat down side by side on a stone bench. He took forever to talk, and my mind percolated in dread, waiting for some doomsday news.

When he finally spoke, I was both surprised and flooded with relief to hear him say that he knew a lot of these Rhodes professors were going to be "way out there liberal," and that I should always remember to not only listen and learn, but to think for myself, because I had a good head on my shoulders. He told me that he knew I would do well, and that he was proud of me. At that point the tears were welling in both our eyes, and my dad finally knew it was time to go. He had said what he needed to say, albeit cloaked in a warning about those crazy liberals: he had faith in me; he was proud of me; I would do well.

That evening, our parents finally gone, Blair and I set off together to have dinner at the Rhodes Refectory (also known as "The Rat"). She had a sincere, earnest way about her, and I liked her immediately. I knew she had gone to a fancy private school in Atlanta, and I was secretly afraid she might be a snob about my own small-town, public school upbringing, but she didn't care about things like that at all. She never has. I don't know of anyone who is more genuine, who values the substance of people over their surface, than Blair.

She is that rarest of person: the kind who would rather listen first. Back in college, our relationship was yin/yang: she was practical and no nonsense; I was a drama queen. A list maker, a schedule keeper, and an invoice organizer, Blair kept our phone bill paid and let me know what I owed her, down to the penny, on little white memo pads.

Our freshman year, she finished her assignments on time, studied well in advance, and didn't procrastinate. I'd pull all-nighters, desperately writing papers I hadn't begun until the day before their due dates, consume Cokes and junk food all night, litter the room with wrappers, then get punchy and wake her up to read my work and bask in its brilliance.

Her side of the room was tidy; its bed, complete with pretty comforter and coordinating sheets, neatly made up each morning. Mine was, well… not. She was indulgent of my messiness, my procrastination, my inconsideration. Looking back, I don't really know why.

She was a bit of a mother hen and worried about my bad habits. Whenever I was stressed over a test I hadn't prepared for and was pulling yet another all-nighter, I would often pull my hair out, strand by strand, hunched over my books and papers. It drove Blair crazy.

"You're going to be bald!" she'd yell, throwing pillows at my head. "You look totally insane!" Eventually she helped me create my "Study 'do"—a tight ponytail that sprouted straight out of the top of my head, à la Pebbles Flintstone. There was no way I could pull my hair out once I had my study 'do firmly in place, and I'm grateful to Blair for, among many things, saving me from baldness.

We lived together for six years—three in college and three in Atlanta after graduation. She is frank in her opinions, often blunt. It can be annoying sometimes, but is mostly refreshing. You know you're getting the unvarnished truth with Blair.

When I was about twenty-three and we were living together in Atlanta, I was hospitalized for two days for a severe allergic reaction. The guy I was dating didn't bother to visit me but called to let me know he would be taking another girl to his Halloween party that weekend due to my illness—but he sure hoped that I "felt better soon!" My boss called to check on me and, once assured that I wasn't dying, briskly informed me that my brochure still needed to get to the printer by deadline, so "perhaps you could just finish a few articles from your hospital bed or, if not, then over the weekend would be fine!"

I remember lying there, feeling miserable and abandoned, indulging in some major self-pity, when Blair walked in the door. She carried a huge pumpkin in her arms and sat it on my wheeled hospital tray. We spent the

> "*The events in our lives happen in a sequence in time, but in their significance to ourselves they find their own order.*"
>
> Eudora Welty

next hour carving a face into it, making a terrific mess, intent on our work. Scooping out pumpkin pulp, I cried a little about the shallow jerk who was dumping me in my hour of need, my insensitive boss, how much the IV had hurt and how the nurses seemed a bit blasé about my (clearly serious) condition. She didn't try to say any of the usual cheer-up stuff, but she didn't need to.

We all need friends who give us sympathy—but we also need those who remind us when it's time to stop wallowing, find our sense of humor or even just our stoic's spine–and carry on. My hospital stay was just a minor upset in life, nothing major, but I'll never forget her smiling face, bringing me that fat pumpkin.

Blair has a way of cutting through the maudlin, which is something that I love. There is, after all, so much of life that is deeply painful. And no one is spared. In the decades that have passed, each of our group of seven has experienced her portion of loss, disappointment, failure, and despair.

Sometimes our losses and regrets are only shared with one friend; sometimes they all come out at once to the entire group during the reunion. Those moments are hard, because you suddenly realize just what she was going through in the last year, many miles away, while you were only seeing the surface emails, the "doing fine" face we all put on for the world when we're just trying to keep going, fighting to stay out of the breakdown lane.

When I asked Blair to tell me a story of a woman who inspired her for this book, I had a feeling that she would choose her mother, Nella, and also that she would want me to write about her beloved father, who she lost in January of our freshman year, so soon after we became roommates and friends.

I remember answering our dorm room phone just a few months before it happened, on a windy day in October. It was her father, calling to say hello. Blair was in class, and I told him I would leave her a message. "Be sure and tell her that her dad loves her and thinks she's beautiful!" he said, and I could hear the smile in his voice.

Blair's story is not only about her mother's resilience in the aftermath of this loss, but also about the sustaining force of her mother's lifelong group of friends. It is a story that echoes, in many ways, the abiding friendship that our own group shares.

*"Had they known at these moments to be quietly joyful? Most likely not. People mostly did not know enough when they were living life that they were living it."*

Elizabeth Strout
*Olive Kitteridge*

# Season of Joy and Sorrow
## Blair's Story

In January of 1982, when I was in the middle of my freshman year at Rhodes College, my handsome, energetic and outgoing father suddenly died at only forty-nine. I was in the midst of what was the happiest, most exhilarating season of my young life—I had done well in my first semester classes and was excited about pledging a sorority. Best of all, I had already made friends at college, real friends.

I didn't know then that those friendships would last a lifetime, didn't ponder such things; but perhaps, unconsciously, I did. What I knew for sure was that I had never laughed so much, or felt such a sense of belonging. The women in this book represent my most enduring friendships, made the year of my terrible loss.

With one phone call, my untroubled world was shattered. I returned home to Atlanta, numb with shock and sorrow. The funeral, visitations, and condolences are a painful, muted blur in my memory. One thing I do recall is how my mother's friends were a constant presence during that time. These were "other moms" I had known my entire life—women my mother, Nella, had forged deep friendships with over her decades as a wife and mother in Atlanta.

> *"What we once enjoyed and deeply loved we can never lose,*
> *for all that we love deeply becomes a part of us."*
> Helen Keller

Our home was filled with women from her Sunday school class at 2nd Ponce de Leon Baptist Church, her tennis partners, her neighbors, and the mothers of my brother's and my friends. They did what women everywhere do when confronted with the worst: they sprang into action, organizing rides to the airport, getting the house in order, preparing food. They simply did what needed to be done.

In the face of death, everything else falls away. But somehow the living must still breathe, eat, and sleep. I don't know how, but those women made sure we did. And no one can provide tangible acts of love and comfort like a Southern woman, usually in the form of chicken casseroles, honey hams, and coconut pies. Looking back, I am deeply grateful for the tender care they took of our small, sorrowful family: my younger brother Hal, my mother, and me.

In spite of my grief, my mother insisted that I return to Memphis quickly after the funeral, and encouraged me to immerse myself in my classes, my sorority, my new friends and interests. She was fierce in her determination that I keep every plan that I had made.

Now I see that she kept my brother and me to our routines because she was afraid that, without its stabilizing influence, Hal and I would dwell in our despair and forever be altered by this early, shocking loss. Her greatest fear was that we would always feel that life was simply too precarious, undependable, and that we could be abandoned at any turn. And if that happened, she would lose us too. Simply put, my Mother wanted us to make an effort for happiness, and not to feel guilty about it.

And so I returned to school. Our weekly phone call became daily, but there was rarely a moment that she didn't sound brisk, even upbeat. She wanted to hear about everything: the Chi Omega formal; my grades; whether or not I had a date that weekend. She spoke about the ordinary, kept the topics prosaic: our dog Bandit's trip to the vet; my brother's college applications; and the thoughtfulness of neighbors who invited her over for barbecues or a hand of bridge on the weekends.

Until I was much older, I didn't know that my Mom cried nearly every day that year; that her despair, sadness, and anger were so overwhelming that she thought she was having a nervous breakdown. Her loyal cadre of friends surrounded her, buoyed her, and carried her to shore, but I doubt if she even showed them the depth of her grief. My mother is a true Steel Magnolia, a believer that one only breaks down in private.

I was making my debut in Atlanta that year, just as my mother had in 1952. The upcoming summer was already scheduled with parties to be hosted and attended, escorts to be arranged, and friends to invite to the festivities. My mother refused to cancel anything. I look back now at the whirlwind of activity and I understand that, even if it might seem trivial, it was healing. It kept us engaged in life.

My mother and I shopped for my white debutante gown together. As I pulled layers of silk chiffon and tulle over my head and modeled dress after dress for her, I could tell that her thoughts were the same as mine: how inconceivable it was that my dad would not be there to escort me to

the dance floor. I would not hold his arm, or feel the warmth of his proud smile as my name was called and we stepped into the ballroom together. But she never acknowledged those thoughts, never said the words aloud, and neither did I.

And so, the following November, as the girls I had grown up with stood in line with their dads; I was escorted by my younger brother. It was hard for me, as I know it was for my mother, to watch my childhood friends swirl past on their fathers' arms. But our loss remained unspoken. My mother wanted us to focus on all we still had, and to be as appreciative as we possibly could of the shining moments before us. That was her way. Looking back, I am grateful for her strength.

Today, more than three decades later, my mother Nella is still the same strong, pragmatic woman. At eighty, she travels to England three times a year to buy furniture and accessories for the antiques business she started with a group of friends two years after my father died. Antiques were something she and my dad had a shared passion for; it was the dream business they had planned to start together after he retired. She was not afraid to pursue that dream on her own.

She has lived alone since 1982, in the same house I grew up in. Her loyal group of friends has lost a few members to illness through the years, but they continue to support one another through good times and bad. My mother is always first on the phone for any of them in times of need, asking what she can do, dropping off groceries and casseroles, giving rides to the airport or the doctor's office, whatever is required. She is organized, no-nonsense, dependable. She is someone to be counted on.

I think of her group of women friends as a kind of cheerful fire brigade, rallying for one another in a way that is the essence of true community and friendship. When my mother broke her leg at age seventy-eight, she didn't want me to fly back to Atlanta to be with her; insisted that she didn't need a fuss, that she was perfectly fine. I flew out anyway. When I got there, I was amazed.

Those same friends and neighbors had created a large calendar in the kitchen on which they had assigned names responsible for driving her to doctors' appointments. Meals were already arriving in a steady, organized procession. She had friends who took turns spending the night with her for months until she was out of the cast. Ever the Southern lady, by the time she had recovered, my mother had written 300 thank-you notes.

She is much loved and she gives much in return. I have often taken her strength for granted, never really thought that she was that remarkable until I was older, and a mother myself; until I had lived long enough to understand just how hard it would be to fully embrace life without a partner to ease its burdens. Now I am in awe of her bravery, independence, and sense of adventure. She did not allow loss to rob her of joy. And thanks to her example and love, neither did I.

Samantha Rivera

*chapter nine*

# Faith

*"It is this belief in a power
larger than myself and other than myself
which allows me to venture into the unknown
and even the unknowable."*

Maya Angelou
*Wouldn't Take Nothing for My Journey Now*

# Kentucky Strong: Loretta and Kela

I am driving through the Kentucky countryside to the tiny farm community of Tompkinsville, population 2,530. It is the first day of June, and all around me the world is the newest green. The rolling hills on either side are dotted with barns, some old and nearly consumed with vines, others sturdy and red. Holstein cows lounge against the edge of a pond, their black-and-white spots graphic against the plush landscape.

The sides of the two-lane road are thick with Queen Anne's lace, purple thistle, and honeysuckle, and I roll my windows down and breathe deeply. It is impossibly beautiful. This drive reminds me of the Kentucky I grew up in, when I'd ride around Logan County with my girlfriends, radio blasting, celebrating the first day of summer.

I am on my way to meet with Loretta Lyons, known affectionately by those close to her as Pearl. Loretta is the mother of Kela Lyons Fee, MD, whom I was lucky enough to call a friend when I was a young mother. Kela's first son and my third were born just a few months apart, and those were colorful and happy years filled with birthday parties and baby showers, Easter egg hunts in the spring and hayrides to the Jackson's Orchard pumpkin patch in the fall.

Even with her demanding schedule as a physician, Kela had so much energy and life that she found a way to make time for it all. She was a woman of boundless love, laughter, faith, and courage, and in everything she did, she shined. She was a beloved wife, mother, daughter, friend, and doctor. And she left this world too soon at the age of forty-three.

Kela and her husband Kirk, an orthopedic surgeon, moved to Bowl-

Samantha Rivera

ing Green in 1997. Within a year, Kela's OB-GYN practice had boomed. Everyone wanted her capable hands to deliver their baby, but it was more than her skill as a physician that drew women to her practice. It is not an overstatement to say that her patients loved her. Several even named their daughters for her. As Loretta put it, "How many women go to see their doctor and get a big ole hug when they come down the hall?" That's the way Kela was: warm, with a wide smile, always going in for the hug. Her love and compassion for people, like her Southern accent, was thick, pure, and authentic.

Like everyone who knew Kela, I felt blessed to have such a person in my life. When she was suddenly diagnosed with stage four cancer at age thirty-nine, our community was shocked that someone with such vibrant energy and purpose could be so sick. For weeks, nearly everywhere I went— my children's school, church, social gatherings—the conversations were the same, hushed and dampened with sadness, fear and incomprehension. Kela's sons were only six and four at the time.

Our entire community mobilized to show support for Kela and Kirk in the only ways we could. Meal preparation and delivery were quickly organized and, with so many people wanting to help in some small way, the schedule was booked months in advance. There were spontaneous prayer vigils at churches, civic and women's groups all over town.

Broadway United Methodist, Kirk and Kela's church home, held a healing service soon after her diagnosis. Word spread throughout Bowling Green and people came from every walk of life, completely filling the church. As my pastor, Rick Bard, describes, "We simply opened the church for people to express their prayers, spontaneous and heartfelt, for Kela and Kirk. The prayers given by new mothers whose babies had been delivered by Kela were especially moving and powerful. I could feel the profound impact Kela had had on these women during the most important experience of their lives. The emotion and love in our church that night was simply beyond words for me."

*"I believe that God is in me as the sun is in the color and fragrance of a flower — the Light in my darkness, the Voice in my silence."*
Helen Keller

Kela and Kirk were on their way back from consulting with cancer specialists in Louisville when they heard about the service. In the midst of all they were dealing with, they drove to the church. Pastor Rick remembers, "I'll never forget seeing them walk in the back doors. There was a hush in the room. I was moved by her bravery, her grace, and the way she hugged and greeted everyone, letting them in to her life, expressing her gratitude for their concern."

Kela was already a person who inspired others, but her dauntless spirit during her four-year battle with cancer gave us all a model for how to live. Knowing Kela made my own faith deeper. When I shared Kela's impact on my spirituality with my Pastor, he responded, "People of courage let us into their lives in a rich way, as Kela did. Perhaps the most powerful face of courage is that which, when faced with the worst, is the simple force of human will that says, 'I will keep going. I will exude hope.'"

And she did. Kela underwent an aggressive treatment of chemotherapy at the James Brown Cancer Center in Louisville. Even though the disease was already widespread, her body responded and scans showed the cancer in complete remission. Kela rejoiced and lived her life even more intensely, taking trips, savoring new experiences, and making memories with her husband and sons. She seemed unstoppable. As other cancer survivors have told me, once you have endured chemo and finally feel good again, the simple absence of pain is something to be cherished and celebrated each day. Not knowing if the cancer would return, Kela left her medical practice to focus on what was most important to her: her family and sharing her faith.

She narrowed her life's focus, but she did not close ranks. Kela viewed her cancer as more than a personal challenge; but as an opportunity to connect with people. She helped raise funds for the James Brown Cancer Center in Louisville, gave speeches to church and civic groups, inspired others with her words, her optimism, her beautiful spirit. She formed Kela's Crew with the Western Kentucky University Women's Volleyball team to raise money for cancer research and treatment.

When she was diagnosed in November of 2004, she was only given about six to eighteen months to live. She lived four years. During that time, she impacted thousands of lives. Dealing with cancer gave Kela a stage to share the strength that was getting her through: her faith in God. As a Christian, she believed in taking whatever came her way in life, no matter how hard, and using it for something good as long as she had breath in her body. This she had learned from her mother, Loretta.

I have often thought about Loretta, and how it would feel to have had such a loving, accomplished, and vibrant daughter, only to lose her so cruelly in the prime of her life. She has been in my prayers many times over the years. When I told Loretta about this book, and how I wanted to write about Kela and the people she inspired, she agreed to meet with me and share her story.

# Loretta Pearl Lyons

After a delicious chicken salad at the City Café in downtown Tompkinsville, where nearly everyone knows Loretta and stops by our table to say hello, I follow behind her in my car to her home. We turn at a sign that reads "Hade's Triple "K" Dairy," and pull up to a pretty white farmhouse. A cow barn is down the hill, silos and a large tractor sit to the right, and flowers bloom in the yard and on the porch. It's peaceful, lovely. She invites me to sit in the cozy front room, surrounded by family photos, and for the next two hours, I am mesmerized by the soft Southern cadences of Loretta Lyons' voice, telling me her story.

Loretta was in her second year at Campbellsville College, working on a teaching degree, when she married the love of her life, Hade Lyons. At that time he was a teacher at a one-room school in Bradley Springs, Kentucky, with dreams of becoming a dairy farmer. After they married, Hade and Loretta lived in a tiny white frame house while she worked to finish her degree and gave birth to their four children: sons Kerry and Kevin, and another son who was born prematurely and died at just two days old. Kela came along in 1965.

Loretta finished college two years later and began her teaching career at Hacker's Branch, another one-room schoolhouse in Monroe County. The next year the one-room schools consolidated, and she started teaching third grade at Tompkinsville Elementary. Not surprisingly, several friends in Bowling Green who attended that school have told me that she was their favorite teacher.

When Hade and Loretta could borrow enough money to realize their dream, they purchased the land for their dairy farm, naming it the Triple "K" Dairy after their children. They were happy, fruitful years, devoted to raising their young family, expanding their dairy farm, and teaching. Listening to Loretta talk, I can hear the joy and satisfaction of those years in her voice, can feel how deeply connected she and Hade were to their community, their church, their land. I am drawn to a grainy, framed photograph of Loretta and Hade, caught in a kiss on a porch swing. They look blissful, carefree.

In 1976, Hade suddenly died of a heart attack at thirty-eight years old. Loretta was only thirty-four. "Losing my husband changed my life in an instant," she tells me. "And in the midst of my grief and sadness – and that of my three children – I also had to decide what to do with the farm. I loved teaching, but I couldn't run the farm on my own and teach full time, too. My dad and Hade's older brother went with me to the lawyer's office soon after Hade died. I remember my dad saying to the lawyer, 'She's gonna have to sell those milk cows.' My heart just hurt at those words. I thought, 'Sell the milk cows?' I knew deep down that I didn't want to do that."

"I got a lot of advice from people telling me to sell the farm, that I couldn't run it on my own with three kids to support. But you know, somehow that just made me more determined to farm. And I couldn't stop thinking about something Hade had told me. I don't know if he thought something was going to happen, but he had said to me once, 'If anything ever happens to me, don't sell the farm until our kids are old enough to decide if they want to farm.' I was just determined to do what I had to do."

And so that summer, Loretta started farming. She set the tobacco and milked the cows. "I worked from daylight to dark, mowing and baling hay, driving the tractors, chopping silage and caring for the livestock. For a while, I think I was doing it to prove that I could, and also to make Hade proud. But it helped me to heal, too. Hard work is the best medicine for healing. That, and having a goal, something to keep you going every day. I'd get into bed and just fall asleep at night."

"The physical work, while exhausting, was actually the easiest part. The tough part was having to make all the decisions alone. I learned as I went along. My husband's older brother was a farmer and he helped me figure things out at first, but eventually he just encouraged me to use my own judgment. I found out quick that farming was a man's world. I'd go to the parts store, or the feed store, or to buy a tractor, and I could tell they thought I didn't know what I was doing. They assumed they could just sell me anything! They were surprised when I told them what kind of bolt I needed and that I knew exactly what type of machinery it was for. They thought there must be a man around somewhere making my decisions for me. Well, there wasn't!"

Kerry, Kevin, and Kela were just fifteen, eleven, and ten at the time of their father's death. "They all had to grow up fast," Loretta acknowledges. "Kerry helped a lot with the farm, and when he graduated high school, he started farming with me full time. Kevin took care of the baby calves, and he was protective. He wouldn't go to bed until everyone else had—and then I'd hear him checking the stove and locking the doors. Kela, just a little girl, started keeping the house and cooking dinner at night, since I worked the farm until dark."

I ask if Kela had always dreamed of becoming a doctor. "Yes she did," Loretta says with a smile. "I remember Hade asking her once when she only seven or eight what she wanted to be when she grew up. She said, in her feisty way, 'I'm gonna be a doctor.' He said, 'Oh good! You'd let momma and me come for free, right?' And she said, 'I would the first time!' We just laughed at that."

I'm not surprised when Loretta tells me that Kela was a whirlwind of activity through her childhood and adolescence. "Kela was always busy doing something. If she was reading a book she was making a potholder at the same time. She studied hard and was the Salutatorian of her class, the class president, and pretty much the president of every other school club or organization! But she never let anything slide. She played the piano for our church on Sundays. She asked her guidance counselor for every scholarship application that came into that high school. Most of them were just getting thrown away and she'd ask if she could take them home. I'd hear her up late every night, filling out applications for scholarship and leadership programs, or making her own clothes. She learned to sew in 4-H and made her own prom dress."

Kela set off for the University of Kentucky on a host of scholarships, the largest of which came from winning the National Miss TEEN Pageant. The pageant recognized young women for their academics, community service, and talent, and contestants were required to either perform or give a speech. Kela wrote a speech that used farming as a metaphor for qualities like patience and perseverance, and delivered it wearing overalls and a straw hat, carrying a crooked neck hoe.

Wearing the same yellow dotted Swiss dress she had sewn for her prom, Kela won the Kentucky Miss TEEN title and flew off to the National Pageant in Albuquerque, New Mexico, with Loretta, who remembers it as an especially happy time. "We sat in her hotel room the night before and read the Bible. I remember telling her, 'If God can get the glory, then I hope you win.' To be honest, we all thought the girl who played the violin was going to win, but she got first runner-up. When Kela's name was called as the winner, we just lost it!"

And that girl who played the violin? She was Gretchen Carlson, who went on to graduate from Stanford, be crowned Miss America, and is today the host of her own Fox News show. But our Kela won the crown that night—not bad for a country girl from Tompkinsville! Even wearing overalls and a straw hat, she shined.

Along with the scholarships, Kela won a trip to Hawaii as Miss TEEN, and Loretta smiles at the memory, telling me how much fun they had together on that adventure. She reminisces in her soft voice about other joyful times: Kela's elated phone call after her acceptance to medical school at the University of Louisville, her beautiful wedding day with a reception in the backyard, the births of her precious sons.

When I ask Loretta to recall when Kela seemed happiest as a child, she says, "The night she was saved. She was the happiest little girl. It was the day after her ninth birthday, and in her testimony before the church she said, 'I didn't think I got much for my birthday this year, but now I got the best present of all.'"

Above all, it was faith that gave Kela her passion for life. It was what grounded her, inspired her, and made her such a radiant presence. She had, after all, watched her mother survive, and then thrive, by leaning hard on God, and never losing faith in His goodness. In the terrible loss of her young husband, Loretta was powerless. But her children needed her. Her farm needed her. She chose to ask for God's help, to draw from His strength, which helped her to become what she needed to be: a powerful woman.

We walk around back, and Loretta shows me her garden, with its lovely outdoor seating area and arbor of purple flowers. She has created a "bottle tree" out of a wooden post skewered with colorful glass bottles of every hue, and she tells me how beautiful it looks illuminated by the rays

of the setting sun each evening. I imagine her sitting in this peaceful spot, with its view of the fields all around, watching her son Kerry and grandson, Hade, driving the tractors and working their land together.

I tell her how much I admire her, how much I learned from the daughter she raised. She smiles and says simply, "I give God all the praise and glory for any good that I might have ever done. I feel like God has blessed me in so many ways. A lot of people don't understand, because of all that has happened. But I think if you let God lead the way, He can take every bad situation and create something good from it. When I think about Kela, it just seems like a dream that she was my daughter. And I think, how did I get so lucky to have a daughter like her?"

# In Memory

In her memory, Kela's husband Kirk had a new baptismal font built for the Ministry and Activity Center of our church. I can feel Kela's sweet spirit whenever I see children baptized there. It is a fitting tribute to a woman of great faith who delivered thousands of new babies.

Last Easter, Pastor Rick Bard spoke about the Baptismal font, and its symbolism for Kela's life, work and faith. "My wife Debbie expressed it beautifully," he said, quoting her. "I've been thinking about the great number of babies that Kela ushered safely into this world. Before a baby is born, the mother's water breaks, and out of the labor and breaking of the water, life comes forth. Every time someone is baptized they go under the water, which represents the death of sin and guilt and regret, and then they are raised up out of the water, which is symbolic of new life and hope through Christ. Every time someone is baptized, I'm reminded that Kela's life is still giving life."

And so am I.

## Consider the Lilies of The Field

Flowers preach to us if we will hear:—
The rose saith in the dewy morn:
I am most fair;
Yet all my loveliness is born
Upon a thorn.
The poppy saith amid the corn:
Let but my scarlet head appear
And I am held in scorn;
Yet juice of subtle virtue lies
Within my cup of curious dyes.
The lilies say: Behold how we
Preach without words of purity.

The violets whisper from the shade
Which their own leaves have made:
Men scent our fragrance on the air,
Yet take no heed
Of humble lessons we would read.
But not alone the fairest flowers:
The merest grass
Along the roadside where we pass,
Lichen and moss and sturdy weed,
Tell of His love who sends the dew.
The rain and sunshine too,
To nourish one small seed.

Christina Rossetti

Joanne Scofield

# chapter ten

# Remember Her

"*We are linked by blood,
and blood is memory without language*"
Joyce Carol Oates

# Silver Charms
# on Invisible Threads

My grandmother loved her charm bracelet. Heavily laden with silver charms, it tinkled irresistibly with every grand gesture she made when telling a good story. With the birth of each grandchild, she added a new charm of a boy's or girl's head in profile, engraved with the celebrated baby's name and birth date. They were the symbols of what was most precious to her, and as a child I loved to watch the shiny charms dance and shiver, always looking for the little girl's head with my name engraved in fancy script.

Perhaps your grandmother had one, too. For centuries, women have worn and loved charm bracelets, not merely as adornment but as a way to honor a precious child or wonderful moment. We celebrate our memories with charms, cast them in gold and silver to keep them near. I suppose we long to make fleeting life feel permanent, if only in symbol. In a way, the beaded evening purse that my grandmother gave me was a charm, too: a talisman to carry into a future that she knew, just knew, was going to shine with all that she hoped for, and prayed for.

My own charm bracelet bears a silver claddagh, the traditional Irish symbol of two hands encircling a crowned heart, representing love, loyalty and friendship. According to Irish tradition, claddagh rings are passed down from mother to oldest daughter or grandmother to granddaughter. My mother tucked this charm in my Christmas stocking many years ago, along with a small card that read, "Remember Her. She loved you so much."

When I said goodbye to my Grandmother and looked at her small body lying in the casket, she was wearing her charm bracelet, her rosary beads in clasped hands. It was the sight of her hands that gave me the strength I needed on that day, for myself and for my mother.

There was always a beautiful, melodious connection between the two of them, and even as a small child, I could see striking shades of my grandmother in my mother. It was as if they were connected by invisible threads, and I was curious whether one day I too would carry the thread. Would I have the same laugh, the same gesturing hands, the same softened eyes when moved by something beautiful?

Some of my earliest, most luminous memories are of seeing their shared happiness as they delighted together over some small thing I had said or done when I was a little girl, their laughter sounding like it came from the same sheet of music. In those moments I could feel the long passage of time and experience beating in my own heart. Somehow I knew, even then, that I would carry with me their parcels of victory and loss.

I was nine years old when we stepped into the airport in New York after living more than two years in Izmir, Turkey, where my father served in the Air Force. My young mother was the picture of 1970s style in her tall black leather boots and swingy wool cape, a jaunty beret angled atop her frosted blonde hair. I thought she was the most beautiful woman in the world, even prettier than the glamorous Pan Am stewardesses we had both admired in whispers to each other on our long flights across Europe.

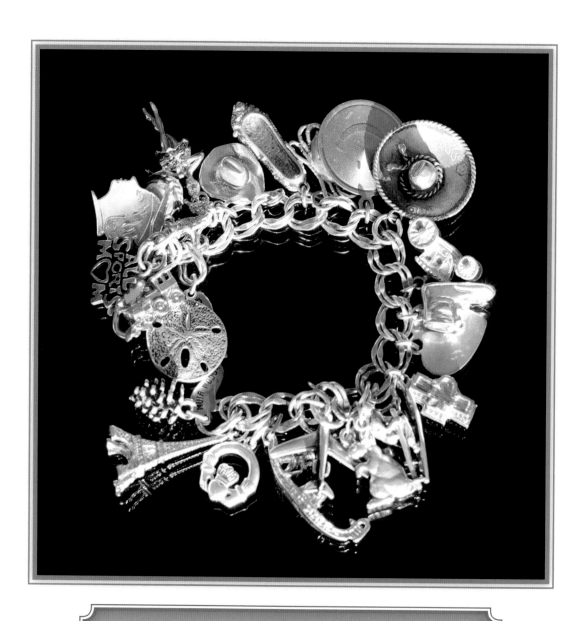

"There is no charm equal to tenderness of heart."
Jane Austen, *Emma*

But it is my grandmother's face that I remember most from my first day home in America. The joy in my grandmother's eyes as she caught sight of my mother was incandescent and it has stayed with me forever, a gift untarnished by years.

As I hung shyly behind my dad and older brothers, I silently watched, mesmerized by the sight of my grandmother's radiant face as she held my mother. Seeing their shared elation brought tears to my eyes, confusing me at such a tender age. "Why am I crying?" I remember thinking. "I'm so happy!" I was far too young to understand tears of joy, but not to experience them.

I remember how Grandma kept pulling back from their embrace so she could better drink in the sight of the daughter who had finally returned from so far away. And I wonder now if my grandmother was thinking of her own mother, whom she never saw again after she sailed away from Ireland as a young girl. "Lillian, you are so beautiful!" She said over and over, her lilting Irish accent made stronger with emotion. "Just look at how gorgeous you are!"

And sometimes, when my mother says the same words to me now, I can see Grandma's face exactly as it was on that reunion day long ago, smiling just behind the veil of my mother's shining eyes.

And I remember her.

## *Remember*

Remember me when I am gone away,
    Gone far away into the silent land;
    When you can no more hold me by the hand,
Nor I half turn to go yet turning stay.
Remember me when no more day by day
    You tell me of our future that you plann'd:
    Only remember me; you understand
It will be late to counsel then or pray.
Yet if you should forget me for a while
    And afterwards remember, do not grieve:
    For if the darkness and corruption leave
    A vestige of the thoughts that once I had,
Better by far you should forget and smile
    Than that you should remember and be sad.

Christina Rossetti